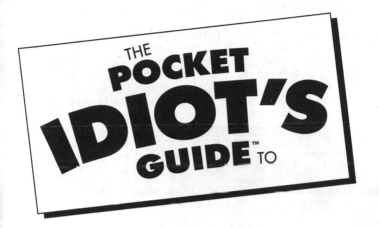

THE POCKET IDIOT'S GUIDE TO

One-Minute Managing

by Arthur R. Pell, Ph.D.

alpha books

A Division of Macmillan General Reference
A Pearson Education Macmillan Company
1633 Broadway, New York, NY 10019-6785

Macmillan Publishing books may be purchased for business or sales promotional use. For information please write: Special Markets Department, Macmillan Publishing USA, 1633 Broadway, New York, NY 10019.

International Standard Book Number: 0-02-863343-1

Library of Congress Catalog Card Number: 99-64050

01 00 99   8 7 6 5 4 3 2 1

Interpretation of the printing code: the rightmost number of the first series of numbers is the year of the book's printing; the rightmost number of the second series of numbers is the number of the book's printing. For example, a printing code of 99-1 shows that the first printing occurred in 1999.

Printed in the United States of America

Note: This publication contains the opinions and ideas of its author. It is intended to provide helpful and informative material on the subject matter covered. It is sold with the understanding that the author and publisher are not engaged in rendering professional services in the book. If the reader requires personal assistance or advice, a competent professional should be consulted.

The author and publisher specifically disclaim any responsibility for any liability, loss or risk, personal or otherwise, which is incurred as a consequence, directly or indirectly, of the use and application of any of the contents of this book.

Alpha Development Team

Publisher
Kathy Nebenhaus

Editorial Director
Gary M. Krebs

Managing Editor
Bob Shuman

Marketing Brand Manager
Felice Primeau

Acquisitions Editor
Jessica Faust

Development Editors
Phil Kitchel
Amy Zavatto

Assistant Editor
Georgette Blau

Production Team

Development Editor
Joan Paterson

Production Editor
Michael Thomas

Cover Designer
Mike Freeland

Photo Editor
Richard H. Fox

Illustrator
Jody P. Schaeffer

Book Designers
Scott Cook and Amy Adams of DesignLab

Indexer
Chris Wilcox

Layout/Proofreading
Angela Calvert
Donna Martin

Contents

1 **Be a Leader—Not a Boss** 1

2 **Goals and Plans** 17

3 **Delegating Work** 31

4 **Hiring the Right People** 43

5 **Effective Interviewing** 59

6 **Equal Employment Laws** 77

7 **Communicating** 97

8 **Motivating** 111

9 **Evaluating Performance** 123

10 **Counseling Employees** 139

11 **Discipline** 157

12 **Separation and Termination** 169

Appendixes

A **Glossary** 185

B **Forms** 195

Index 197

Introduction

The world is changing, and management is changing with it. Whether you're starting your first assignment as a team leader or have years of experience, you have to keep up with these changes. Ideas that weren't even dreams a few years ago are now part and parcel of the corporate culture.

In this book, you'll discover how the team concept will enable you to take advantage of the skills, brains, and creativity of every person on your team. We look at the myths and misconceptions that have often dictated management style. Then we examine approaches to setting goals and developing channels of communication to make sure that your ideas and instructions are understood and accepted by your team members. You'll also learn techniques to encourage team members to contribute ideas and suggestions about every aspect of their work.

To keep you abreast of the requirements of the Equal Employment Opportunity laws, I have included a list of pre-employment questions you can and cannot ask. Special attention is given to the latest developments in this area, including the Americans with Disabilities Act and how to avoid sexual-harassment complaints.

The day-to-day problems that leaders face on the job, including dealing with poor performance, poor conduct, and alcohol and drug addiction are covered. You'll learn how to counsel employees and when and how to refer them to professionals for help. Last, you'll learn how to apply progressive discipline when warranted and how to terminate employees legally and tactfully. We will also explore voluntary separations and how to reduce turnover. You will learn about the concept of "employment at will" and what it means to you as a manager.

You will find shaded boxes throughout the book that can help you understand and implement the material in each chapter:

Meanings and Gleanings

Definitions to clarify and highlight many of the terms used in the chapter.

Secret Weapon

Practical tips and techniques to help you accomplish some of the ideas in the book.

Trademarks

All terms mentioned in this book that are known to be or are suspected of being trademarks or service marks have been appropriately capitalized. Alpha books and Macmillan General Reference cannot attest to the accuracy of this information. Use of a term in this book should not be regarded as affecting the validity of any trademark or service mark.

Chapter 1

Be a Leader—Not a Boss

In This Chapter

➤ Developing team synergy

➤ Learning how to lead rather than boss

➤ Evaluating your management style

➤ Debunking myths about management

You've been managing people for years. You think that you know the ins and outs of running your department, but your boss says that you're not meeting the company's goals. You're cautioned to "get up-to-date or get out." You think, "I'm doing okay—the boss is being unreasonable." Or perhaps you've just been promoted to your first supervisory job. Your boss congratulates you, shakes your hand, and says "Take over." No training, no advice—just "take over." It's nice to get the promotion, but don't you wish that you could get some training?

What happens if the people who report directly to you or your team members are giving you a hard time? No matter how hard you try to get them to do their work, to meet deadlines, or to comply with quality standards, they do just enough to keep from getting fired. Stop blaming others. Look to yourself. Are you managing like a 19th-century autocrat or like a 21st-century leader? Take a look at how your approach to management shapes up with what the management gurus consider the "right way." Sure, you're entitled to your opinion, but keep an open mind. You want to do a better job—that's why you're reading this book.

Agree or disagree with the statements in the "Test Your Managerial Skills" section of this chapter to take inventory of how you manage now. Then compare your answers with the answers following the inventory.

Don't Dictate—Facilitate

Men and women in today's corporate environment do not respond to authoritative styles. Truly successful managers commit themselves to obtaining the willing cooperation of all involved. They are facilitators who make every effort to make things go smoothly for their staff or team.

Secret Weapon

Don't be afraid to try new approaches. The management climate is changing. To keep up with it and to make progress, you have to take risks.

Most people respond best to leaders who treat them as adults, encourage them to make suggestions about their work, and listen to their ideas even when those ideas may disagree with their own. Successful leaders encourage people to be contributors rather than just order-takers.

Working in Teams

To experience the greatest success in getting people to co-operate willingly, use the team approach. What is a team? Most people would answer, "It's a group of people working to achieve a common goal." That's a good answer, but not good enough. Even if groups work together to achieve a common goal, it does not make them a team. There's much more to it.

Team Synergy

A key word must be added to this definition: *synergy*. A team is a group of people working synergistically to achieve a common goal. When people work together collaboratively as a team, each one benefits from the knowledge, work, and support of each of the other team members, which leads to much greater productivity than would be achieved by each person working at top capacity as an individual.

Meanings and Gleanings

When a team has **synergy,** the whole is greater than the sum of its parts (2 + 2 may equal more than 4).

A good example of synergy is a rocket ship, which is made up of a series of components (stages). For the ship to function, each component must be in tiptop condition. But even if all components are in A-1 shape, the rocket still won't get off the launch pad unless all components work together interactively, or synergistically.

You are the rocket engineer; your team members are the components. To make that team effective, you must ensure that each member works at optimum capacity and that the members work collaboratively to achieve the synergy that will lift your project from its launch pad to its successful completion.

From Group to Team

Molding a group of people into a team involves more than just changing each person's title from "employee" to "associate" or "team member." *Your own attitude is the key to success.* When you act as a facilitator (as a coordinator or leader) rather than as a boss, your staff members begin to feel like—and then act like—team members.

Building your team requires careful planning. No team can just spring up by itself. You must work carefully with team members to explain several factors:

> ➤ How they are expected to work.

> ➤ How this new method of operation differs from what they are used to doing.

> ➤ Where they can go for help.

> ➤ How the new team approach works.

Giving just lip service to the team approach doesn't work—you must "walk the talk." You must change your way of dealing with problems as they occur. Rather than make decisions arbitrarily, encourage team members to come up with solutions to problems and to implement those solutions. You should guide and facilitate rather than direct the work of your team.

Secret Weapon

Handling certain tasks is no longer your job: You can't do it all by yourself. Help your team members to develop their skills, and then give them the ball and let them run with it.

Test Your Managerial Skills

The following inventory will help you assess your management style. Read each statement and check the appropriate box beside each question to indicate whether you agree or disagree with each statement. Then compare your responses to the answers that follow.

Statement	Agree	Disagree
1. It isn't necessary for a manager to discuss long-range goals with team-member subordinates. As long as team members are aware of the immediate objective, they can do their work effectively.	❏	❏
2. The best way to make a reprimand effective is to dress down an offender in front of coworkers.	❏	❏
3. Managers show ignorance and risk loss of face if they answer a question with, "I don't know, but I'll find out and let you know."	❏	❏
4. It pays off for a manager to spend a great deal of time with a new employee to ensure that training has been effective.	❏	❏

continues

continued

Statement	Agree	Disagree
5. Managers should ask their associates for their ideas about work methods.	❏	❏
6. When discipline is required, you should be careful to avoid saying or doing something that may cause resentment.	❏	❏
7. People will work best for a tough manager.	❏	❏
8. It is more important for a team to be composed of members who like their job than of people who do it well.	❏	❏
9. The work gets done most efficiently if a manager lays out a plan in great detail.	❏	❏
10. For a manager to lead an effective team, the feelings, attitudes, and ideas of team members should be kept in mind.	❏	❏

Okay, you've answered all the questions. Now look at the responses based on the advice of successful managers:

1. **Disagree.** Persons who know where they are going—who can visualize the long-range picture—are more committed to reaching those objectives and will work harder to attain them.

2. **Disagree.** Dressing a person down does not solve the problem—it only makes the person feel small in front of coworkers. A good reprimand corrects a

problem without humiliating the person. It is best to reprimand in private—never in front of others.

3. **Disagree.** It is better to admit ignorance of a matter than to try to bluff. People respect leaders who accept that they don't know everything.

4. **Agree.** The most important step in developing the full capabilities of associates is good training on the part of managers. Managers who invest the time in the beginning will lay the foundation for developing each newcomer into a valuable asset of the organization.

5. **Agree.** Persons directly involved with the job often can contribute good ideas toward the solution of problems they are close to.

6. **Agree.** Resentment creates low morale and often leads to conscious or subconscious sabotage.

7. **Disagree.** Tough is not as important as fair and inspiring.

8. **Disagree.** The happiness and satisfaction of team members on the job are important, but they are secondary to getting the job done.

9. **Disagree.** Psychologists have shown that most people work better when they are given broad project guidelines and can work out the details themselves. An exception is that some people do work better when tasks are given to them in detail. A good manager recognizes the styles in which people work and adapts to them in dealing with each person.

10. **Agree.** Communication is a two-way street. To manage effectively, it's important to know what team members are thinking and how they feel about the job.

There is no passing or failing score for this inventory. Its purpose is to make you think about how you manage people. You may not agree with all the answers, but at least pay them some heed. Most of what you find here is discussed in detail later in this book.

Myths and Misconceptions

Myths and misconceptions that have governed people's thinking for years (for a lifetime, in many cases) are tough to overcome. As a manager, however, you must shatter them if you want to be able to move ahead.

Secret Weapon

Leadership is an art that can be acquired. You can learn to guide people in a way that commands their respect, confidence, and whole-hearted cooperation.

Many managers like to refer to themselves as "professionals," but is management really a profession? Professionals in other industries (such as physicians, lawyers, psychologists, and engineers) are required to complete advanced study and pass exams for certification. Some managers may have special education—for instance, degrees in business administration—but *most managers are promoted from the ranks and have little or no training in management*. Most managers learn primarily on the job.

More successful managers are making an effort to acquire skills through structured courses of study, but most managers still pick up their techniques by observing those of their bosses. The model they follow may be good. Too often, however, new managers are exposed to their bosses' outdated and invalid philosophies. Let's look at some of the many myths and misconceptions about management.

Management = Common Sense

One manager said, "When I was promoted to my first management job, I asked a longtime manager for some tips about how to deal with people who report to me. He told me, 'Just use common sense and you'll have no trouble.'"

What is "common sense," exactly? What appears to be sensible to one person may be nonsense to another. Often the definition of "common sense" is culturally based. In Japan, for example, it's considered "common sense" to wait for a full consensus before making any decision; in the United States, this technique is often derided as a waste of time. Culture aside, different people also have their own ideas about what is good or bad, what is efficient or wasteful, and what works and what doesn't.

We tend to use our own experiences to develop our particular brands of common sense. The problem is, a person's individual experience provides only limited perspective. Although what we think of as common sense has been developed from our own experiences, an individual's experience is never enough to provide anything other than limited perspectives. Leadership involves much more than the experience an individual may have. To be a real leader, you must look beyond common sense.

You wouldn't rely solely on common sense to help with financial or manufacturing problems. You would call on the best possible expertise in these areas for advice and information. Why then should you resort to a less pragmatic base in handling human-relations problems?

You can learn a lot about the art and science of management by reading industry-related books and periodicals, attending courses and seminars, and actively participating in trade associations in your industry.

Managers Know Everything

Managers don't know everything. Nobody does. Accept that you don't have all the answers. But know that you need the skills to get the answers. If you get to know people in other companies who have faced similar situations, you can learn a great deal from them. Networking gives you access to these people when you need new information and ideas, and provides you with a valuable ongoing resource for assistance in solving problems.

Meanings and Gleanings

One of the fastest-growing phenomena of the past decade is *total-quality management.* In this system, a company focuses entirely on the production of high-quality products or services.

Benchmarking is a process of seeking organizations that have achieved success in an area and learning about their techniques and methods.

Seeking organizations that have been successful in certain areas and learning their techniques is called *benchmarking.* One of the peripheral benefits of the total-quality movement has been the practice of benchmarking: seeking organizations that have been successful in certain areas and learning their techniques. Companies that participate in competitions such as the Malcolm Baldrige Awards (presented annually by the U.S. Department of Commerce to firms that have demonstrated high quality in their work) must agree to share their techniques with any organization that requests this information. Benchmarking is one of the peripheral benefits of *total-quality management.*

It's My Way or the Highway!

Management by fear is still a common practice. People will work if they fear that they might lose their jobs, but how much work will they do? The answer is "Just enough to keep from getting fired." That's why this technique isn't considered effective management. Successful management involves getting the *willing* cooperation of your associates.

Moreover, it's not that easy to fire people. Considering the implications of the civil rights laws and labor unions—and in many cases the difficulty and costs associated with hiring competent replacements—firing people may cause more problems than keeping employees with whom you're not satisfied.

You can't keep good workers for long when you manage by fear. When jobs are scarce in your community or industry, workers might tolerate high-handed, arbitrary bosses. But when the job market opens up, the best people will leave for companies with more pleasant working environments. Employee turnover can be expensive and often devastating.

Don't Believe in Praising

People need to be praised. Everyone wants to know that his or her good work is appreciated. Yet many managers are reluctant to praise their employees. Why? Some managers fear that if they praise a team member's work, that person will become complacent and stop trying to improve (certainly, some people do react this way). The key is to phrase your praise in a manner that encourages the team member to continue the good work.

Other managers are concerned that if team members are praised for good work, they will expect pay raises or bonuses. And some folks might. But that's no reason to withhold praise when it's warranted. Employees should already know how salary adjustments, bonuses, and other financial rewards are determined. If compensation is renegotiated at annual performance evaluations, team members should be assured that the good work for which they are praised will be considered in the evaluation.

Some managers simply don't believe in praise. One department head told me, "The people I supervise know that they're doing okay if I don't talk to them. If I have to speak to them, they know they're in trouble." Offering no feedback other than reprimands isn't effective, either. Remember, you want to use positive, not negative, reinforcement.

Secret Weapon

Praise can be overdone. If people are repeatedly praised for every trivial accomplishment, the value of praise is diminished to the point of becoming superficial. Also, a nonproductive employee can think he's doing great if he is praised excessively.

K.I.T.A. (Kick in the *You-Know-What*)

Sure, some managers still kick their employees in the rear end—not literally, but verbally. Every year James Miller, management consultant and the author of *The Corporate Coach,* holds a contest for the Best and Worst Boss of the Year. The employees do the nominating. Miller reports that he gets many more nominations for worst boss than for best boss. One of the chief reasons employees dislike their bosses, Miller found, is that the bosses use verbal K.I.T.A.s—continually finding fault with subordinates, expressing sarcasm, gloating over failures, and frequently hollering and screaming at employees.

We all raise our voices occasionally, especially when we're under stress. Sometimes it takes great self-discipline *not* to yell. Effective leaders, however, control this tendency. An occasional lapse is okay, but when yelling becomes your normal manner of communication, you're admitting your failure to be a real leader. You cannot get the *willing* cooperation of your associates by screaming at them.

Try the Platinum Rule

When you manage people, the Biblical rule "Do unto others as you would have others do unto you" is sound advice—to a point. Because people are *not* all alike, treating others as *you* want to be treated is not the same as treating them as *they* want to be treated.

For example, Linda prefers to be given broad objectives and likes to work out the details of her job on her own. But her assistant, Jason, is not comfortable receiving an assignment unless all the details are spelled out for him. If Linda delegates work to her assistant in the way she likes to have work assigned to her, she won't get the best results.

Sol needs continuous reinforcement. He's happy on the job only when his boss oversees his work and assures Sol that he's doing a good job. Tanya, however, gets upset if her boss checks her work too often. "Doesn't she trust me?" she complains. You can't do unto Tanya as you do unto Sol and get good results from each of them.

Each of us has our own style, our own approach, and our own eccentricities. To "do unto others" as we would have them do unto us may be the poorest way of managing people. To be an effective manager, you must know each member of your team and tailor your method of management to each person's individuality. Rather than follow the golden rule, follow the *platinum* rule: "Do unto others as they would have you do unto them."

Compromises must be made, of course. In some situations, work must be done in a manner that may not be ideal for some people. By knowing ahead of time what needs to be accomplished, you can anticipate problems and prepare team members to accept their tasks.

Meanings and Gleanings

When you work with your associates, rather than follow the golden rule, remember the *platinum rule:* Do unto others as they would have you do unto them.

Production, Performance, Profit, and People Potential

Production, performance, and profit are important aspects of your job as a manager, but are these all you have to consider? Certainly, if a business is to survive, it must produce results. Equally important, however, is the development of its employees. If you ignore people's potential, your team's ability to achieve results is limited. Instead, you reap short-term benefits at the expense of long-term success and even survival.

When Sam Lee founded his computer-components company, he was a pioneer in what was then a new and growing industry. Determined to be a leader in his field, he drove his employees to maintain high levels of productivity and kept his eye carefully trained on the profit picture. But he paid no attention to the development of his staff. His technical and administrative staff members were given little opportunity to contribute ideas or use their own initiative on their own projects. Over the years, Lee's company saw reasonable profits, but it never grew to become an industry leader as Lee had hoped. Because he had stifled the potential and ambition of his employees, he lost many of his technical staff members to other companies. And because he depended only on his own ideas, he missed out on all the innovative ideas his staff might have come up with.

Chapter 2

Goals and Plans

In This Chapter

➤ Setting realistic and attainable goals

➤ Developing standards with SOPs

➤ Planning for the long haul

➤ Scheduling day-to-day activities

The first steps toward becoming a modern manager begin when you set goals. Like a good navigator, you determine how and when you want to reach those goals. Some people like to set out on a journey without a map. They want to ride the currents and hope that they'll find adventure and fortune—but managers can't afford to take those risks. Because managers have responsibilities to their teams, they must know where they want to go, what they want to accomplish, what kinds of problems they may encounter along the way, and how to overcome those problems.

Plant Your Goal Posts

Unless you know exactly what you want to achieve, there's no way to measure how close you are to achieving it. Specific goals give you a standard against which to measure your progress. The goals you set for accomplishing your team's mission must be in line with the larger goals your company sets for you. If you don't coordinate the objectives of what you plan to achieve for your job, department, or team with the objectives of your organization, you'll waste your time and energy.

Goals are the foundation of motivational programs. In striving to reach your goals, you become motivated. In knowing the goals of your team members and helping them reach those goals, you help to motivate them. In most organizations, overall big-picture goals are established by top management and filtered down to departments or teams, who use them as guides in establishing their own goals.

Goals Are More Than Hopes

The process of setting *goals* takes time, energy, and effort. Goals aren't something you scribble on a napkin during a your coffee break. You must plan what you truly want to accomplish, establish timetables, determine who will be responsible for which aspect of the job, and then anticipate and plan a resolution for any obstacles that may threaten to thwart the achievement of your goals.

Meanings and Gleanings

Goals and *objectives* are interchangeable terms that describe the purpose, or long-term results, toward which an organization's or individual's endeavors are directed.

Pipe Dreams or Goals?

Are you ready to set your goals? To prevent them from being mere pipe dreams, be sure that they meet the following three conditions:

1. **Clear and specific.** It's not enough to state that your goal is "to improve the market share of our product." Be specific (for example: "Market share of our product will increase from its current 12 percent to 20 percent in five years.").

2. **Attainable.** Pie-in-the-sky goals are self-defeating. If you can see yourself getting closer to attaining your goal, you'll have more incentive to continue working than if your goals seem completely impossible to achieve.

3. **Flexible.** Sometimes you just can't reach a goal. Circumstances may change: What once seemed to be viable may no longer be. Don't be frustrated.

Here's a lesson in flexibility: An assistant manager set a goal to become a store manager in two years, but it didn't happen. Rather than quit his job in frustration, he reviewed his situation. He had based his goal on the premise that his company would continue to open six to ten new stores every year. During the preceding year, business had been slow, and only two new outlets were opened. But business improved, and the company seemed likely to renew its expansion. He recognized that quitting would be the wrong solution and that he had to be flexible in the time limits he set for himself.

Changing Goals with Changing Circumstances

All of us set goals based on certain circumstances we anticipate during the life of a project. Circumstances do change, however, and original goals may have to be adjusted. To anticipate that end, many companies use a goal-setting program that involves three levels:

➤ **A main, or standard, goal:** What you plan to accomplish if everything goes well.

➤ **Alternative 1:** A slightly lower goal. If circumstances change and it becomes obvious that your main goal cannot be achieved, rather than start from scratch in redefining your goal, you can shift to this alternative.

➤ **Alternative 2:** A higher-level goal. If you're making greater progress than you had originally thought you could, rather than be complacent about being ahead of target, shift to this alternative and accomplish even more.

Take, for example, CSC, a company in the metropolitan Philadelphia area that services and repairs computers. Its sales goal for one year was to open ten new accounts. To prevent loss of customers when a national competitor opened a service outlet in the same community, all the company's energies were redirected toward saving its current accounts. The goal for attracting new clients then had to be reduced.

Let's say that if CSC was having a good year, its goals could have been accelerated. If CSC had gained eight new clients in the first half of the year, it could have automatically raised its goal to a higher level.

Getting the Team to Buy into the Goal-Setting Process

At a recent goal-setting seminar, one participant complained, "I have trouble getting people to buy into the big-picture concept. They're so absorbed in their individual jobs that they can't see beyond their own problems." Here's how you can overcome this type of situation:

> Bring everyone in your department or on your project team into the early stages of the planning process.

> Discuss the major points of the overall plan.

> Ask each person to describe how he or she will fit into the big-picture plan.

> Give each person a chance to comment on each stage of the project.

Breaking a long-term goal into bite-size pieces that people can relate to can help them to see how their part in a project fits together with the other parts. They can also then see how to set overall team or project goals for the long run.

SOPs: The Company Bible

Your company may have a set of standard operating procedures (SOPs), or standard practices (SPs), that detail company plans and policies. Although progressive companies usually restrict their SOPs to such matters as personnel policies, safety measures, and related matters, many companies either incorporate specific job methods and procedures into their "bibles" or publish them in accompanying "instruction manuals." Providing policies and procedures for routine activities eliminates the need to plan anew for them every time they occur. Because SOPs set standards that everyone must follow, all employees working with the manuals can refer to them at any time, which ensures consistency in dealing with particular situations.

If you have to develop SOPs, keep them simple. SOPs too often become complicated because of managers' desires to cover every possible contingency. *It can't be done.* Managers frequently have to make decisions based on many unforeseeable factors. SOPs should cover the common issues in detail, but leave room for managers (or nonmanagerial people, where appropriate) to make spontaneous decisions when circumstances warrant them.

SOPs should also be flexible. Plans may become obsolete because of new technologies, competition, government regulations, or the development of more efficient methods. Build into SOPs a policy for periodic review and adjustment.

Keep in mind that not all plans are SOPs. Plans may be developed for special purposes, sometimes to be used only once, and sometimes for projects that last several months or even years.

Secret Weapon

A Guide to Successful SOPs: Clearly state any expected actions; Specify where deviations are not permitted; Provide guidelines for acceptable deviations; Test the SOP before making it final.

Planning at the Team Level

Your entire team should be involved in developing the team's plans. As team leader, you should coordinate and lead the process: Assign particular aspects of the planning to the team members who are the most knowledgeable about them, coordinate the process, and make decisions that have a significant effect on the entire project.

Professional Planners

Because many line managers are so bogged down in the day-to-day details of the job, they don't have the time and energy for planning. Because planning is so important, many organizations have planning specialists work with the managers in developing and coordinating this function. The people who are closest to the work—those who will be responsible for implementing the plans—should also be directly involved in the planning process. Planning experts can help facilitate the process, but only the people who will carry out the project's duties can create a realistic and workable plan.

How to Plan

To illustrate how planning works, let's look at how Louise, the owner and manager of Featherdusters (a janitorial service company in Rock Hill, South Carolina), developed a plan to take over a new account to clean a six-story office building. The following list shows you the steps that Louise deemed necessary to implement her plan:

Step 1: List what needs to be done. After consulting with her client, Louise made the following list:

Must be done daily	Must be done weekly
Empty wastebaskets into dumpsters	Sanitize telephones
Carry dumpsters to pick-up location	Polish brass railings
Dust furniture	Wax tile floors
Mop tile floors	
Vacuum carpeted floors	
Clean restrooms	
Clean lounges	

Must be done monthly
Wash windows
Wash glass partitions

Step 2: Determine staffing. Louise hired two teams of three people, one of them a working supervisor. Each team was responsible for cleaning three floors and was comprised of a trained floor waxer, a window washer, and a supervisor. The owner/manager oversaw the entire operation.

Step 3: Acquire supplies and equipment. Louise then acquired these supplies: vacuum cleaners, dust cloths, sponges, a waxing machine, floor wax, disinfectant, and window-washing solvent.

Step 4: Estimate timing. Louise calculated that the cleaning job would take five hours (from 5 p.m. to 10 p.m.) five days a week to complete. The following list serves as a guide to Louise and the supervisors to ensure that scheduled tasks get done at the scheduled time:

➤ **Daily tasks:** All daily tasks are performed daily.

➤ **Weekly tasks:** The supervisor assigns one floor every day to one or more workers to complete each of the weekly tasks.

➤ **Monthly tasks:** The owner/manager and window washer schedule these tasks every month. The schedule must be flexible enough to account for weather conditions.

Step 5: Methods. All work will be performed according to the company's SOP for cleaning methods. Supervisors are responsible for quality of work, and the owner/manager will inspect work on an ad-hoc basis.

Step 6: Budget. Specific figures should be included to cover cost of materials, equipment amortization, labor, transportation to and from the site, and miscellaneous costs.

Step 7: Contingencies. Things don't always work out according to plan. Unforeseen circumstances can develop that impede the completion of scheduled tasks. Louise anticipated the types of contingencies most likely to be encountered:

➤ **Truck or van breakdown:** Make arrangements for renting replacement vehicles.

➤ **Equipment breakdown:** Additional waxing machines are stored in a warehouse.

➤ **Personnel:** Owner/manager and supervisors have lists of substitutes who are available on short notice.

Step 8: Follow-up. Owner/manager makes periodic visits to the site to inspect work and meets at least once per quarter with the client to ensure satisfaction with the work.

The following planning worksheet enables you to systematically plan and schedule the projects you undertake. Feel free to photocopy it or adapt it to meet your special needs.

Planning Worksheet

Objective: _____

Specific actions to be taken: _____
_____
_____

Staffing: _____
_____

Equipment and supplies: _____
_____

Timing (include deadlines where required): _____
_____
_____

Methods and techniques to be used: _____
_____
_____

Budget: _____
_____
_____

Contingencies: _____
_____
_____

Follow-up: _____
_____
_____

Converting Plans into Action

The introduction of a new product requires a much more complex plan. It may involve phase-by-phase components spread out over several months or even years. For example, when Proctor and Gamble (P&G) introduced Crest toothpaste to the market, it set up separate yearlong plans for each of the main aspects of the project: manufacturing, marketing, and distribution. The product manager who coordinated the entire operation then developed, in collaboration with the manufacturing, marketing, and distribution managers in each of these functions, month-by-month plans. Each of the involved parties knew just what it had to accomplish in the specified period and were kept informed of each other's progress. Every effort was made to keep the project on target. By following this plan, P&G was able to introduce Crest toothpaste on time. Simultaneously, P&G supplied its retailers, placed ads on TV and in magazines, and mailed samples and discount coupons to consumers.

Planning for Daily Activities

You'll achieve your goals only if you break down, day by day, how you plan to reach them. Whether you have participated in the planning or the plan was handed down to you, scheduling the work is essential to getting it accomplished. Unless the work you do is primarily routine and standardized schedules are in the SOPs, the next step for you and your team members is to determine when and what task each member will undertake.

The $25,000 Suggestion

In the early 1900s, Ivy Lee, a pioneer in management consulting, paid a visit to Charles Schwab, then the president of U.S. Steel. Lee told Schwab that he could help U.S. Steel become more effective. When Schwab expressed skepticism, Lee said, "I'll give you one suggestion today, and I want you to put it into effect for one month. At the end of that time, we will meet again, and you can pay me whatever you think that idea was worth to you. If it was of no value, you owe me nothing."

Schwab accepted the challenge and implemented Lee's suggestion. When they met again, Schwab handed Lee a check for $25,000. He said, "That was the best advice I ever had. It worked so well for me that I passed it on to all my subordinate managers."

So, what was Lee's advice? *Prioritize.*

Secret Weapon

Set priorities and stick to them. When you're interrupted, deal with the interruption and then immediately get back to what you were doing.

Every morning when you get to work (or you may prefer to do it at the end of the previous workday), make a list of all the things you want to accomplish that day and put them in order of priority. Then work on the first item, and don't move on to the next one until you have done all you can. You'll be interrupted, of course—no job is free from interruption—so just handle the interruption and then return to what you were working on. Don't let any interruption make you forget what you were doing. You probably won't have completed every item on your list at the end of the day. But the important tasks will have been accomplished. Take the remaining tasks, add them to the new ones that have developed, and compile another pri-oritized list for the next day. At the end of the month, you might notice some items may have remained on your list day after day. That's a sign that they weren't important enough to do. You should either delegate them to some-one else or perhaps not do them at all.

What Do I Do First?

In his book *The Seven Habits of Highly Effective People,*
Stephen Covey cautions that many managers confuse
what is *urgent* with what is *important.* Urgent matters must
be attended to immediately or else serious consequences
might ensue. But if you spend all your time putting out
fires, your truly important goals won't be met.

Scheduling Team Projects

After your team has planned the actions it will take to
complete a project, you must develop a schedule. Lay out
what will be done, who will do it, and when each task
should be started and completed. Your schedule can be
as simple as notes on a wall calendar, or as complex as
specially designed planning charts or computer-based
schedules. The daily planning organizer below breaks
down activities into categories.

Daily Planning Organizer

Date: _____

Priorities	Things to Do	Phone Calls
Correspondence	Appointments	Miscellaneous

*A planning organizer helps your team schedule daily activities
and achieve its goals.*

You can print the planner on loose-leaf paper and keep it in a binder, or you can blow it up to use as a wall chart. You can also format it for computer use. Color-code your calendar or planning chart so that you and your associates can tell at a glance the status of projects and assignments. **Red ink:** High-priority items for that day. **Blue ink:** Deadlines for projects (list in blue for two or three days before the actual deadline, then print in red on the day of the final deadline). **Green ink:** Follow-up of other people's work. **Black ink:** Routine work scheduled for that day.

Chapter 3

Delegating Work

JILL- THE McSMITH ACCOUNT,
BOB- SALES
JOE- APPLICATIONS...

WORK SCHEDULE

In This Chapter

➤ Overcoming your fears of delegating

➤ Understanding the five elements of effective assigning

➤ Scheduling the workload

➤ Managing multiple priorities

Your team has lots of work to do. What will you do yourself? What will you assign to other team members? When you delegate, you assign to others not only tasks but also the power, and the authority, to accomplish them. Effective delegation means that a team leader has enough confidence in his or her team members to know that they'll carry out an assignment satisfactorily and expeditiously.

Don't Hesitate—Delegate!

Sure, you're responsible for everything that goes on in your department or team, but if you try to do everything yourself, you'll put in twelve or more hours a day. There are some certain things, of course, that only you can do, decisions that only you can make, critical areas that only you can handle. That's where you earn your keep. Many of the activities you undertake, however, can and should be done by others. This list discusses some of the reasons you may hesitate to *delegate* and explains why you should reconsider:

➤ **You can do it better than your associates.** That may be the case, but you should spend your time and energy on more important things. Each of your team members has talents and skills that contribute to your team's performance. By delegating assignments, you give the team members the opportunity to use those skills.

How often have you thought, "By the time I tell a coworker what to do, demonstrate how to do it, check the work, find it wrong, and have it done over, I could have completed it myself and gone on to other things"? Showing someone how to perform a certain task will take time now, of course, but after your coworker masters the task, it will make your job easier later.

➤ **You get a great deal of satisfaction from a certain aspect of the work and hesitate to give it up.** You're not alone. All of us enjoy certain things about our work and are reluctant to assign them to others. Look at the tasks objectively. Even if you have a pet project, you must delegate it if your time can be spent handling other activities that are now your responsibility as a manager.

➤ **You're concerned that, if you don't do it yourself, it won't get done right.** You have a right to be concerned. But there is a way to ensure that it will be done properly.

Now that you are convinced of the value of delegating, follow these five principles to guide your team members along the path to productivity.

Meanings and Gleanings

Delegation enables you to position the right work at the right responsibility level, helping both you and your team members expand skills and contributions. You also ensure that all work gets done on time by the right person who has the right experience or interest.

One: Who's Gonna Do the Work?

You know the capabilities of each of your associates. When you plan their assignments, consider which person can do which job most effectively. If you're under no time pressure, you can use the assignment to build up another person's skills. The more team members who have the capabilities to take on a variety of assignments, the easier your job is for you. If no one on your staff can do the work, then of course you'll have to do it yourself. You should train one or more team members in several areas so that you can delegate work in those areas when necessary.

Two: Tell 'em What to Do

After you give detailed instructions to one of your team members, your usual question is probably "Do you understand?" And the usual answer is "Yes." But does the employee really understand? Perhaps that person isn't quite sure, but in good faith says "I understand." Or maybe the person doesn't understand at all but is too embarrassed to say so. Rather than ask "Do you understand?" ask "What are you going to do?" If the response indicates that one or more of your points isn't clear, you can correct it before the employee does something wrong.

When it's essential for an employee to rigidly conform to your instructions, make sure that he or she thoroughly understands them. Give a quiz. Ask specific questions so that both you and your team member completely agree about what he or she will do. When it's not essential for a delegated activity to be performed in a specific manner, you can just get some general feedback.

Tailor the way you make *assignments* to the preferences of the person to whom you're delegating. Some people like to have responsibilities spelled out explicitly, perhaps in the form of a written list of items. Others prefer more general instructions. Some people prefer e-mail, and others would rather have you delegate in person.

Meanings and Gleanings

Some people use the word *assigning* when they're talking about short-term projects and the word *delegating* for long-term projects. The terms are usually interchangeable.

Three: Understand and Accept

Your instructions must be both understood *and* accepted by your team member. Suppose that on Tuesday morning, Janet, the office manager, gives an assignment to Jeremy with a deadline of 3:30 that afternoon. Jeremy looks at the amount of work involved and says to himself, "There's no way!" It's unlikely that he will meet that deadline.

To gain acceptance, let your team member know just how important the work is. Janet might say, "Jeremy, this report must be on the director's desk when she comes in tomorrow morning. She needs it for an early-morning meeting with the executive committee. When do you think I can have it?" Jeremy may think, "This is important. If I skip my break and don't call my girlfriend, I can have it by 5:00."

Why did Janet originally indicate that she wanted the report by 3:30 when she didn't even need it until the following morning? Maybe she thought that if she said 3:30, Jeremy would knock himself out and finish the report by the end of the day. But most people don't react that way. Faced with what they consider to be an unreasonable deadline, most people won't even try. By letting people set their own schedules within reasonable limits, you get their full commitment to meeting or beating a deadline.

But suppose that Janet really did need to have that report by 3:30—so that it could be proofread, photocopied, collated, and bound. To get the report completed on time, she could have assigned someone to help Jeremy or allowed him to work overtime.

Be realistic when you assign deadlines. Don't make a practice of asking for projects to be completed earlier than you need them, because they won't be—people will stop taking your deadlines seriously.

Secret Weapon

To ensure that projects are completed when you need them, set a realistic completion date, or deadline.

Four: Control Points

A control point is the point at which you stop a project, examine the work that has been completed, and, if errors have been made, correct them. Control points can help you catch errors before they blow up into catastrophes. A control point is *not* a surprise inspection. Team members should know exactly when each control point is established and what should be accomplished by then.

Suppose Gary, a team leader, gives a project to Kim on Monday morning. The deadline is the following Friday at 3:00 p.m. They agree that the first control point will be at 4:00 p.m. Tuesday, at which time Kim should have completed parts A and B. Notice that Kim knows exactly *what* and *when*. When Gary and Kim meet on Tuesday, they find several errors in part B. That's not good, but it's not terrible. The errors can be corrected before the work continues. If Gary and Kim had not scheduled a control point, the errors would have been perpetuated throughout the entire project.

Five: Provide the Right Tools and the Authority

You can't do a job without the proper tools or the authority to get the job done. Providing equipment, computer software, and access to resources is an obvious step, but giving away authority is another story. Many managers are reluctant to give up any of their authority. If a job is to be done without your micromanagement, you must give the people doing the job the power to make decisions.

If they need supplies or materials, give them a budget so that they can order what they need without having to ask for your approval for every purchase. If a job might call for overtime, give them the authority to order it. If you have to be around to make every decision, the work will get bogged down.

Secret Weapon

Don't micromanage. You'll stifle creativity and prevent team members from working at their full potential.

Team or workgroup members almost always have questions, seek advice, and need your help. Be there for them, but don't let them throw the entire project back at you. Let them know that you're available to help, advise, and support, but not to do their work.

Putting Delegation to Work

Now that you know about the principles of delegation, you're ready to apply them on the job. To help you systematize your approach to delegation, use the sample worksheet "Getting Your Team to Work Together" (see the inside back cover). You may photocopy it or adapt it to your needs.

Secret Weapon

When people bring you a problem, insist that they bring with it a suggested solution. Train them to solve their own problems and not constantly bother you with small things.

Delegating to Teams

When an organization is structured into teams, work should be delegated and assigned as a team activity. When the people who will do the job have some control over the assignments they get, they approach their work with enthusiasm and commitment.

When your boss gives you a complex project, present it in its entirety to your team. Discuss with your team how to break the assignment into phases. Delegating each of the phases to individual team members will follow easily. Most members will choose to handle the areas in which they have the most expertise. If two members want the same area, let them iron it out with each other. But if it gets sticky, you should step in and resolve the problem diplomatically. Certain phases of the assignment are bound to be tough or unpleasant. No one's really going to volunteer to do them. Have your team set up an equitable system for assigning this type of work.

Secret Weapon

If you have a difficult task, assign it to a capable but lazy person. He or she will find an easy way to do it.

As team leader, be sure that every member of your team is aware of not only his or her own responsibilities but also of everyone else's responsibilities. In this way, everyone knows what everyone else is doing and what kind of support he or she can give to or receive from others. To keep everyone informed, create a chart listing each phase of the assignment, the person handling it, deadlines, and other pertinent information. Post the chart in the office for easy reference.

Delegating to Multidepartmental Teams

When a job requires coordination among many diverse workgroups within a company, use a *multidepartmental team*. An effective team has these characteristics:

➤ It is composed of representatives from all relevant internal departments, such as sales and production. Team members are usually chosen by the team leader in coordination with managers of the various involved departments.

➤ Outside representatives, such as customers, suppliers, and subcontractors, are invited to participate in team discussions. Although these people aren't members of the team, their input is important in helping the team accomplish its goal.

Meanings and Gleanings

In a *multidepartmental team*, also called a *cross-functional team*, representatives from different departments are temporarily assigned to work collaboratively on a project.

➤ Production schedules are determined based on customers' needs. Team members are given detailed information about these needs and are encouraged to deal directly with customers to keep up-to-date on necessary adjustments.

➤ Delivery of materials is arranged on a just-in-time basis. To avoid unnecessary inventory costs, arrangements are made for delivery of materials and supplies as close as possible to the time they'll be used.

➤ Work assignments are planned collaboratively and control points are established. Some projects require teams to meet daily to coordinate and maintain attention to the assignment. Other projects require only occasional meetings to check on progress and deal with problems.

The key to the success of multidepartmental programs is communication. Team members are encouraged to communicate in person, on the telephone, or by writing, faxing, or e-mailing each other on a timely basis. Problems can then be addressed without delay.

Managing Multiple Priorities

If you're a typical manager, you're probably loaded down with more work than it seems possible to do—and so are your team members. Darlene, for example, is not only working on a project for you but is also on the quality-assurance team and is involved in the research for a new product. Hans, a member of your functional team, has been asked to work on a special project for another manager. All these assignments are important, but you're responsible for getting the work accomplished on your project.

What can you do when members of your team have other assignments that are equally important or when your team is facing several high-priority tasks that must be completed in the same time frame? Putting in more hours, bringing more work home, and going to the office on weekends may help, but it often results in stress, fatigue, and low morale, which can reduce performance and productivity. Don't forget that most people have families, other interests, and the need to rest and refuel.

Communicate, Communicate, Communicate

You can't pull rank. It used to be that you could force your priorities on others because you were higher on the totem pole. Occasionally, this is still acceptable, but in most progressive organizations such power plays are discouraged.

Work it out. Talk to team members and to other team leaders to schedule work that will enable all of you to make the best contribution you can to your organization. This process takes diplomacy and a willingness to compromise.

Work Smarter—Not Harder

A limited number of hours is available for work, and no matter how you look at it, there are only 24 hours in a day. For most managers, the eight-hour workday is a mere pipe dream. Many people spend ten or more hours at the office and then take work home with them at night. Overwork does exist. In the past few years, as more and more companies have downsized, overworking has become a serious problem. Employees who remain in an organization after a downsizing have to take on their ex-colleagues' assignments in addition to their own workload.

You should seek new and creative approaches to your work—work smarter, not harder. Ask yourself: Which kind of work can be eliminated? Which work processes can be reengineered? Which can be delegated? The time you spend learning about new approaches will pay off through expedient performance.

Secret Weapon

When you say "no" to an assignment, explain how taking on the assignment would inhibit completion of other higher-priority projects. Suggest alternative solutions.

Don't Be Afraid to Say No

You can't do everything. At times, your team gets so bogged down with work that taking on another assignment would simply be impossible. How can you turn it down diplomatically?

Sometimes you can't. The project may have a high priority and must be completed. In that case, reexamine all your other projects. Determine which of them can be put on the back burner until you can complete the new assignment. Some projects may be ahead of schedule and can be temporarily postponed; others may not be as important as the new job. Discuss these issues with your boss and work together to reschedule other priorities.

Often, you can just reschedule. The new assignment may not be a high-priority project and can be put on hold for a while. Or maybe the project can be done more effectively by another team. It's no shame to admit that your group may not have the necessary background for a project. Know your limitations.

Chapter 4

Hiring the Right People

In This Chapter

➤ Making a job analysis

➤ Matching job specs to a job description

➤ Finding applicants in a tight job market

➤ Screening résumés and applications

➤ Studying applications and résumés

Suppose that you have an opening in your department. You want to fill that position with a person who has the necessary skills to perform the required duties of the job and who can contribute to the success of your team. Before you can even begin searching for this person, however, you had better have a clear and realistic concept of what you need.

Maybe you're seeking to fill the position of a person who has left your team, and you may already have a job description for that job. The easy way is just to use the existing job description, but that's not necessarily the best way. This is your chance to review the description in light

of the changes that may have developed since it was originally written. Reanalyze the job. Treat it as though it were
a brand-new position. In this way, the new job description
will reflect the current duties and activities of the job.

Making a Job Analysis

The specialists who perform *job analyses* may be industrial
engineers, systems analysts, or members of your human
resources staff. If your company employs these people, use
them as a resource. The best people to make an analysis,
however, are those closest to a job—you and your team
members. A job analysis should include a written description of the responsibilities that fall within a job (*job description*) and a written description of the skills and background
required to perform a job effectively (*job specification*).

Meanings and Gleanings

When you perform a *job analysis*, you determine the duties,
functions, and responsibilities of a job (the *job description*)
and the requirements for the successful performance of
that job (the *job specifications*).

Four Techniques for Developing a Job Description

To make a realistic job description, follow these guidelines:

1. **Observe.** For jobs that are primarily physical in nature, watching a person perform the job will give
   you most of the material you need to write the description. If several people are engaged in the same
   type of work, observe more than one performer.

   Even a good observer, however, may not understand
   what he or she is observing. Sometimes the job

involves much more than meets the eye. In jobs that are not primarily manual, however, there is little that you can learn from observation alone. Just watching someone sitting at a computer terminal, for example, isn't enough to learn what's being done.

2. **Question the performer.** Ask the people who perform a job to describe the activities they perform. This technique fleshes out what you're observing. You must know enough about the work, of course, to be able to understand what is being said and to be able to ask appropriate questions. It's a good idea to prepare a series of questions in advance.

3. **Question the supervisor or team leader.** If you are the team leader, review in your mind how you view the position, what you believe the performer should be doing, and the standards that are acceptable. If you're analyzing a job other than the ones you supervise, speak to the team leader or supervisor to obtain that person's perspective on the position.

4. **Make it a team project.** When work is performed by a team, job descriptions cover the work of the entire team. The best way to develop a complete job description is to get your entire team into the act.

Secret Weapon

Don't base your job specifications on your vision of an ideal team member. Specs should reflect what you believe a person should bring to the job that will contribute to the team's successful performance.

The job-description worksheet is a helpful tool. It should cover these categories: Job title; Reports to; Duties performed; Equipment used; Skills used; Leadership responsibility; Responsibility for equipment; Responsibility for money; Other aspects of job; Special working conditions; and Performance standards. Tailor the form you use to the type of job you're analyzing.

The Specs: What You Seek in a Candidate

After you know just what a job entails, you can determine which qualities you seek in the person who will be assigned to do the job. Most job specifications include these elements:

➤ **Education.** Does a job call for college? Advanced education? Schooling in a special skill?

➤ **Skills.** Must the candidate be skilled in computers? Machinery? Drafting? Statistics? Technical work? Any of the skills necessary to perform a job?

➤ **Work experience.** What is the type and duration of previous experience in related job functions?

➤ **Personal characteristics.** Does a candidate have the necessary skills in communication, interpersonal relations, and patience? Does he or she have the ability to do heavy lifting?

Secret Weapon

Don't clone your current team. Keep in mind that your team will be stronger if it includes people with different, but complementary, skills.

Job specs can be so rigid that you're unable to find anyone who meets all your requirements. Sometimes you have to make compromises. Reexamine the job specs and set priorities. Consider the following examples where flexibility in meeting job specs is important.

1. **Which of the specs are nonnegotiable?**

   Examples: In civil service jobs or in cases in which job specs are part of a union contract, even a slight variation from job specs can have legal implications. An accountant making formal audits must be a certified public accountant (CPA). An engineer who approves structural plans must be licensed as a professional engineer (PE). A truck driver candidate must have a license to drive a semitrailer and a machinist candidate must be able to do machine work to precise tolerances.

2. **Which of the specs are important but not critical?**

   Examples: Although having a CPA degree may be a good credential, an internal auditor doesn't have to be certified. Although the specs for a job require knowledge of certain software, experience with different but similar software might do almost as well.

3. **If there's no compelling reason for the candidate to have a specific qualification**, you may deviate from the specs and accept an equivalent type of background.

   Example: Suppose that your specs call for sales experience but an applicant has no job experience in selling. As a volunteer, however, she was a top fundraiser for the local community theater. That person may be able to do the job.

In seeking to fill a job, a team leader should make every effort to meet the job specs, but should also have the authority to use his or her judgment to determine when deviation from the job specs is acceptable.

Secret Weapon

The intangibles that make for success on a job are just as important as education, skills, and experience. Be as diligent in determining the intangible factors as you are with the tangible factors.

What Do I Have to Pay to Get the Person I Need?

Another part of job analysis involves determining the pay scale for a job. Most organizations have a formal job-classification system in which various factors are weighed to determine the value of a job. These factors include

➤ Level of responsibility

➤ Contribution of a job to a company's bottom line

➤ Type of education

➤ Training and experience necessary to perform the job

Notice that the classification applies to a job, not to the person performing a job.

The pricing of a job in smaller organizations is often done haphazardly: You pay what you have to pay in order to hire the person you want. You have to determine the "going rate" for a job you want to fill.

Recruiting Personnel

You have a job opening on your team, and you've prepared the job description and job specs. Now you're ready to screen applicants. The first thing you should do is contact your human-resources department. The HR team is composed of experts in recruiting and choosing personnel and usually takes care of most of the initial steps in the hiring procedure. The HR department can provide you with advice that can save you time and effort involved in the part of the hiring process you do yourself. An important part of their responsibility is that they're aware of all the legal implications involved in this delicate area and can help you avoid problems.

Your Best Bet May Be Close By

People who already work for your company may make valuable members of your team. They may work at jobs in which they don't use their full potential, or they may be ready for new challenges. Joining your team would be a move up for them.

Taking Advantage of Internal Transfers

Not every transfer is a promotion, but it's often an opportunity for someone to learn, gain experience, and take a step forward in preparing for career advancement. Seeking to fill a team vacancy from within a company has many advantages:

➤ People who already work in your company know the "lay of the land." They're familiar with your company's rules and regulations, customs and culture, and practices and idiosyncrasies. Hiring these people rather than someone from outside your company saves time in orientation and minimizes the risks of dissatisfaction with your company.

➤ You know more about these people than you can possibly learn about outsiders. You may have worked directly with a certain person or observed him or her in action. You can get detailed and honest information about a candidate from previous supervisors and company records.

➤ Offering opportunities to current employees boosts morale and serves as an incentive for them to perform at their highest level.

➤ An important side effect is that it creates a positive image of your company in the industry and in your community. This image encourages good people to apply when jobs for outsiders do become available.

Limitations of Promoting Only from Within

Although the advantages of internal promotion usually outweigh the limitations, there are disadvantages to consider:

➤ If you promote only from within, you limit the sources from which to draw candidates and you may be restricted to promoting a person significantly less qualified than someone from outside your company.

➤ People who have worked in other companies bring with them new and different ideas and know-how that can benefit your team.

➤ Outsiders look at your activities with a fresh view, not tainted by over-familiarity.

Where Are the Applicants?

In addition to searching for candidates within your company, the HR department may help you *recruit* from outside sources. It may advertise the opening, contact employment services, visit colleges (for trainees), or use executive recruiters (often called "headhunters") for higher-level positions.

Before the actual recruiting begins, the team leader and the members of the HR team review the job specifications to coordinate the process. As expert as HR people may be in their specialty, however, they cannot do the job alone. A team leader's knowledge of the job and the team's personality is necessary to ensure that the best-qualified candidates are sought out and considered.

In one recent poll, 53 percent of employees surveyed said they expected to leave their current employer voluntarily within the next five years. In such an environment, the ability to recruit and retain the most qualified workers is essential. Simply running a classified ad or calling an employment agency is no longer enough to attract good employees. To cope with a job market in which there is a shortage of good workers, managers must use the best resources available to them and create new, innovative approaches.

Push the HR Department

If you work for a large organization, chances are that you do not do your own recruiting. You work through the human-resources or personnel department. Naturally, you're not their only client. Other team leaders and managers are pestering them to fill their job openings. In this job market, they have their hands full. Here are some suggestions:

➤ Make friends with the HR staff—not just when you need people, but as a regular practice. If you haven't done this up to now, it may be too late for your current needs, but work on it, and next time you have a job to fill, you'll see the difference.

➤ Offer to help them by contacting people you know. For example, you may be a member of a professional association and can tap its resources.

➤ Offer to screen résumés from ads. This saves them time and work, and you will have to look at them sooner or later, anyway.

➤ Give them prompt reactions to anybody they refer to you. One of the biggest gripes HR people have about team leaders is their stalling about making decisions.

Routine Sources for Job Applicants

If you work for a company that does not have a human-resources or personnel department, you may have to dig up candidates on your own. Even if a job is hard to fill, don't overlook the standard sources for recruiting applicants. These are tried-and-true methods.

➤ **Help-wanted ads.** The most usual source for hiring is to place ads in local newspapers for routine jobs. These ads are read by local residents who are seeking positions. However, if your job is hard to fill and you are willing to relocate people from other areas, your best bet is to advertise in trade or professional journals.

➤ **Private employment agencies.** Most of these agencies have files of applicants who are immediately available and can match them against your job specs, enabling you to fill the job quickly. Because they screen applicants before referring them, you will see only qualified people and avoid the wasted time of interviewing countless unqualified people.

Contact employment agencies that specialize in your type of work. You can identify these agencies by studying the ads that they place in newspapers and professional journals. If they cover a variety of jobs in your areas of interest, they may know people who fit your needs. Once you have established a relationship with one or two agencies, you will have a ready source of personnel when needed. Most employment agencies require the employer to pay a fee, which may range from 10 to 20 percent of the annual salary paid to the employee, and even more for technical and management jobs.

➤ **Headhunters.** Executive or technical recruiters differ from employment agencies in that they put their efforts into identifying and going after specific candidates, who are usually currently employed and not actively seeking jobs. These firms usually work on only higher-paying positions. Some firms charge a flat fee, paid whether they fill the job or not; most take a nonrefundable retainer and a percentage of the salary if they succeed in filling the job.

➤ **State employment services.** Each state has an employment or job service that can recommend applicants for your jobs. You certainly should list your jobs with the local office of this agency. State services also often provide testing and other screening facilities. Some companies have developed excellent relations with these agencies. Other firms have expressed dissatisfaction because state placement services are primarily concerned with finding jobs for unemployed people and will not be able to refer good candidates who are currently employed and not registered with them.

➤ **School-affiliated employment services.** High school, college, and technical or specialized school employment services are excellent sources for recruiting people with little or no experience. Most do not charge a fee and are anxious to place their graduates. (Some schools training people in jobs for which graduates are in short supply do charge fees.) These schools sometimes will also refer alumni who do have work experience.

Finding Qualified People for Hard-to-Fill Jobs

Your first move is to tap the resources you have on hand—your current staff. Most people in technical and other specialized work have friends and acquaintances in their own fields. They belong to professional associations, keep up with classmates, and attend conventions. Ask them for referrals. Some companies have formal programs in which rewards are given for referrals that result in a hire. Another source is to contact the placement committees of appropriate professional associations.

Surf the Internet

If your company doesn't have a Web page, get one. This is a particularly effective tool for recruiting computer specialists and other technically trained people. There are also several Web sites that carry classified ads or even match applicants with job openings (for a fee).

Attend Job Fairs

These are sometimes organized by trade associations or private recruiting firms. They tend to specialize in specific types of jobs. Companies may rent a booth at the fair to attract the applicants, provide them people with job information, and even conduct preliminary interviews.

Train People

Another approach is to hire willing and adaptable people and train them in the particular skills required to do the jobs. Some firms seek graduates of community colleges, vocational schools, and high-school graduates who don't plan to go to college and train them for entry-level positions.

Seek Out Retirees, Part–Time, and Share–Time Workers

Some employers are asking retirees if they would consider working part-time; others are luring mothers of young children back to the workforce early by helping with day care. Others arrange for two people to share a job—each person working part-time. This allows for continuity in the work and gets jobs done that must be done. These methods, usually used by people who need time for family responsibilities, bring to the company talents that would have been lost if full-time work was demanded.

Screening Résumés

You may receive hundreds of résumés in response to an ad. It can take hours and hours of your time to read them and make your preliminary judgments. Not only can you save time, but you can uncover hidden problems in the résumés by following these guidelines:

➤ Establish some "knock-out factors." These are job requirements that are absolutely essential to performing the job. They include necessary educational qualifications and/or licenses. For example, a degree in electronics, a plumber's certification, or an airplane pilot's license.

➤ Select key aspects of the job and screen for them. When you have many applicants for a position, you can narrow the field by looking for experience in those key aspects.

➤ Look for gaps in dates. Many people who have had short-duration jobs leave them out of their résumé. Some signs to watch for are the following:

1. Specifying years only rather than month and year (for example, 1996–1999 for one job and 1991–1996 for the previous job). It may mean only a short period of unemployment between jobs, but it may also mean that a job held for several months between the listed jobs was omitted.

2. Listing the number of years worked instead of dates. This may also be a cover-up for gaps in work history. And it could also indicate the applicant's attempt to emphasize older jobs when his or her more recent work experience is not relevant to the job being sought. For example, say the job sought is market analyst. The applicant was a market analyst ten years ago, but has been working in a different type

of position since then. By placing the marketing experience first on the résumé and not specifying dates, the impression is that the marketing job was most recent.

3. Giving more space on a résumé to older positions. This may be due to the applicant simply updating an old résumé instead of creating a new one—which could be a sign of laziness. Or it may just mean that the more recent jobs were of lesser pertinence than previous ones.

4. Overemphasis on education for experienced applicants. If a person is out of school five or more years, the résumé should primarily cover work experience. What was done in high school or college is secondary to what has been accomplished on the job. For such applicants, information about education should be limited to degrees and specialized programs completed.

None of these is necessarily a knock-out factor. They simply suggest further exploration in the interview.

Secret Weapon

Use a résumé as a supplement to an application, not as a substitute for it.

All Candidates Should Complete an Application Form

In addition to résumés, most companies require all applicants to complete an application form. Résumés are an applicant's sales pitch—designed to make you want to hire him or her. A résumé can hide undesirable aspects of a person's background or overplay positive factors. An application form provides you with the information *you* need to know, not what the applicant wants you to know.

Because all the information requested on the application form is the same for all applicants, it complies with the equal-employment-opportunity laws. In addition, it helps you compare applicants' backgrounds when you make your hiring decision. Make sure that all applicants complete the form, even if they provide a detailed résumé. Study an application to get a better idea about a candidate's background before you call the person in for an interview.

Secret Weapon

Make sure that your application form meets EEO guidelines. Have your legal department or an attorney who specializes in labor law review your application before you have it printed.

Chapter 5

Effective Interviewing

In This Chapter

➤ Preparing to give an interview

➤ Conducting the interview

➤ Giving tests and checking references

➤ Making good hiring decisions

An interview shouldn't consist of just a casual conversation: You should be prepared to ask questions that enable you to judge an applicant's qualifications and give you insight into that person's strengths and limitations as they apply to the job.

Preparing for an Interview

To ensure that you get the information you want, make a list of pertinent questions *before* you meet with a candidate:

1. **Review the job description.** Prepare questions that bring out an applicant's background and experience in the functions of that job.

2. **Review the job specifications.** Prepare questions to help you evaluate whether an applicant's background and skills conform with what you're seeking.

3. **Review a person's application and résumé.** Some of the information you need may be gleaned from these documents. Prepare questions that expand on what's in those documents.

Questions You Should Ask

Structure interviews so that you don't forget to ask important questions. You usually should explore the five areas in this list:

1. **Education.** Does an applicant meet the educational requirements or have other background experiences that would provide the necessary technical know-how?

2. **Experience.** Inquire about the type and length of pertinent experience. Ask not only "What did you do?" but also "How did you do it?" You can determine from an applicant's answers whether he or she has the type of experience that's necessary for a job.

3. **Accomplishments.** It's important to learn what an applicant has done to make him or her stand out from other qualified candidates.

4. **Skills.** Learn which special skills an applicant can bring to a job.

5. **Personal characteristics.** The job specifications should indicate the personal characteristics necessary for doing a job. During an interview, try to identify, in addition to these characteristics, other personality factors that may affect the applicant's compatibility with you and your team members.

The following list of interview questions can guide you in preparing the questions you want to ask a job candidate.

Interview Questions

Work Experience

(Add specific questions to determine job knowledge and experience in various aspects of the job for which you are interviewing.)

Describe your current responsibilities and duties.

How do you spend an average day?

How did you change the content of your job from when you started it until now?

Discuss some of the problems you encountered on the job.

What do you consider to be your primary accomplishment in your current job (or in previous jobs)?

Qualifications Other than Work Experience (helpful questions for applicants with no direct work experience)

How do you view the job for which you are applying?

What in your background particularly qualifies you to do this job?

If you were hired, in which areas could you contribute immediately?

In which areas would you need additional training?

In what way has your education and training prepared you for this job?

Weaknesses

In which aspects of your previous job did you perform best?

In which areas did you need help or guidance from your boss?

In which areas of your work have your supervisors complimented you?

Motivation

Why did you choose this career area?

What do you seek in a job?

What's your long-term career objective?

How do you plan to reach this goal?

Of all the aspects of your last job (or jobs), what did you like most? Least?

What kind of position do you see yourself in five years from now?

What are you looking for in this job that you're not getting from your current job?

Stability

What were your reasons for leaving each of your previous jobs?

Why are you seeking a job now?

What were your original career goals?

How have these goals changed over the years?

Resourcefulness

Describe some of the more difficult problems you have encountered in your work.

How did you solve those problems?

To whom did you go for counsel when you couldn't handle a problem yourself?

What's your greatest disappointment so far in your life?

In what way did this disappointment change your life?

Working with Others

On what teams or committees have you served?

What was your function on this team (or committee)?

What did you contribute to the team's activities?

How much of your work did you do on your own? As part of a team?

Which aspect did you enjoy more—working alone or as part of a team? Why?

What did you like best about working on a team? Least?

Secret Weapon

Don't limit yourself to the questions on the list. Listen to the answers—not only to what an applicant says but also to what he or she *doesn't* say. Follow up with probing questions.

Conducting an Interview

Most job applicants are nervous or at least somewhat ill-at-ease in an interview. Welcome applicants with a friendly greeting, a smile, and a handshake, and offer a cup of coffee or tea. Introduce yourself and begin the discussion with a noncontroversial comment or question based on something from an applicant's background. After you "break the ice," you're ready to move into the crux of an interview and ask the questions you have prepared.

Secret Weapon

Elicit from applicants information about what they have done in previous jobs (or other areas of their lives) of which they're particularly proud. Past successes are good indicators of future achievements.

Is the Applicant Holding Something Back?

Have you ever had the feeling that an applicant is hiding something or is reluctant to talk about a particular aspect of his or her background? These three techniques may help open these closed doors:

1. **Use silence.** Most people cannot tolerate silence. If you don't respond after the applicant has finished talking, he or she will usually fill in the gap by adding something more. "I have experience in mass-mailing software." [Silence.] "I did it once."

2. **Make nondirective comments.** Ask open-ended questions, such as, "Tell me about your computer background." An applicant will tell you whatever he or she feels is an appropriate response. Rather than

comment on the answer, respond with "Uh-huh" or "Yes," or just nod. This technique encourages applicants to continue talking without giving any hints about what you're seeking to learn. This approach often results in obtaining information about problems, personality factors, attitudes, or weaknesses that might not have been uncovered by direct questions. Conversely, it can also bring out additional positive factors and strengths.

3. **Probing questions.** Sometimes applicants can be vague or evasive in answering questions. Probe for more detail, as in this example:

INTERVIEWER: For what types of purchases did you have authority to make final decisions?

APPLICANT: Well, I know a great deal about valves.

INTERVIEWER: Did you buy the valves?

APPLICANT: I recommended which valves to buy.

INTERVIEWER: Who actually negotiated the deal?

APPLICANT: My boss.

Secret Weapon

After a response, *wait five seconds before asking your next question.* You'll be amazed at the new information—positive or negative—that is added to the original response.

Is the Applicant Trying to Dominate the Interview?

Have you ever interviewed an applicant who tried to take over the interview? Instead of answering your questions, he tells you what he wants you to hear. Sometimes the applicant will rephrase your question so he can answer it in a manner favorable to him. For example, you ask: "Tell me about your experience selling to department store buyers." The response: "Department store buyers are not as difficult to deal with as small-store owners." The interviewee then expands on his experience in that market.

To overcome this, when the applicant pauses for breath, quickly interrupt by rephrasing the original question. "I see your point, but what experience have you had selling to department store buyers?"

Take Pertinent Notes

Take brief notes during an interview and record the highlights. Write down enough information so you'll remember who each applicant is, what makes one applicant different from another, how each applicant measures up to the job specs of the position for which she or he has been interviewed, and, of course, the decision you made. Taking detailed notes during an interview often makes an applicant "freeze up" and, if you're busy writing, you can't fully listen.

Secret Weapon

Before making a hiring decision, have an applicant interviewed by other people who will work closely with that person.

In the case of investigations by federal or state EEO agencies, good records of an interview can be your most important defense tool. When records are unavailable or inadequate records have been kept, the opinion of the hearing officer is based on the company's word against the word of an applicant. Complete and consistent records give your company solid evidence in case of an investigation.

Employment Tests

Do tests help in choosing employees? Some companies swear by testing; others swear at them. In companies in which tests are used extensively as part of the screening process, the HR department or an independent testing organization does the testing. Except for performance tests, it's unlikely that you will have to administer tests.

The most frequently used tests in hiring are the following:

➤ **Intelligence tests.** Measure the person's ability to learn. They vary from brief, simple exercises (such as Wunderlich tests) that can be administered by people with little training to highly sophisticated tests that must be administered by someone who has a Ph.D. in psychology.

➤ **Aptitude tests.** Determine the potential of candidates in specific areas, such as mechanical ability, clerical skills, and sales potential. Such tests are helpful in screening inexperienced people to determine whether they have the aptitude in the type of work for which you plan to train them. Most aptitude tests can be administered and scored by following a simple instruction sheet.

➤ **Performance tests.** Measure how well candidates can do the job for which they apply. Examples include operating a lathe, entering data into a computer, writing advertising copy, and proofreading manuscripts. When job performance cannot be tested directly, written or oral tests on job knowledge may be used. You must give the same test in the same manner to all applicants. In a word-processing test, for example, you must always use the same material, the same type of computer, and the same time frame.

➤ **Personality tests.** Designed to identify personality characteristics, they vary from the Readers Digest quickie questionnaires to highly sophisticated psychological evaluations. Supervisors and team leaders are cautioned not to make decisions based on the results of personality tests unless the full implications are made clear to them by experts. You can obtain information about approved tests from the American Psychological Association, 750 First St., Washington, DC 20002; (202) 336-5500.

Verifying References

Unless your company policy requires that reference checks be made by the human-resources department, it's better for you, the team leader, to do it. You have more insight into your team's needs and can react to the responses to your questions with follow-up questions that will help you determine whether the applicant's background fits your needs. Be careful to follow the same guidelines in asking questions of the reference as you do in interviewing applicants. Just as you can't ask an applicant whether she has young children, for example, you can't attempt to get this type of information from the reference.

Getting Useful Information from a Reference

Most reference checks are made by telephone. To make the best of a difficult situation, you must carefully plan the reference check and use diplomacy in conducting it.

➤ **Call an applicant's immediate supervisor.** Try to avoid speaking to the company's HR staff members. The only information they usually have is what's on file. An immediate supervisor can give you details about exactly how that person worked, in addition to his or her personality factors and other significant traits.

➤ **Begin your conversation with a friendly greeting.**
Then ask whether the employer can verify some information about the applicant. Most people don't mind verifying data. Ask a few verification questions about dates of employment, job title, and other items from the application.

➤ **Diplomatically shift to a question that requires a substantive answer,** but not one that calls for opinion. Respond with a comment about the answer, as in this example:

You: Tell me about her duties in dealing with customers.

Supervisor: [Gives details of the applicant's work.]

You: That's very important in the job she is seeking because she'll be on the phone with customers much of the time.

By commenting about what you have learned, you make the interchange a conversation—not an interrogation. You're making telephone friends with the former supervisor. You're building up a relationship that will make him or her more likely to give opinions about an applicant's work performance, attitudes, and other valuable information.

Making the Decision

The interviewing is over and references have been checked. You now have to decide which candidate to hire. Before you make a decision, review the evaluations of all the people who interviewed applicants. Discuss the finalists with your team members and others who may have interviewed them.

Decision-Making Boo-Boos

In making a hiring decision, make every effort to avoid letting irrelevant or insignificant factors influence you. These factors include:

➤ **Overemphasizing appearance.** Although neatness and grooming are good indicators of personal work habits, good looks are too often overemphasized in employment. This bias has resulted in companies rejecting well-qualified men and women in favor of their more physically attractive competitors.

➤ **Giving preference to people like you.** You may subconsciously favor people who attended the same school you did, who come from similar ethnic backgrounds, or who travel in the same circles as you.

➤ **Succumbing to the halo effect.** Because one quality of an applicant is outstanding, you overlook that person's faults or attribute unwarranted assets to him or her. Because Sheila's test score in computer know-how is the highest you've ever seen, for example, you're so impressed that you offer her a job. Only later do you learn that she doesn't qualify in several other key aspects of the job.

In making a final decision, carefully compare each candidate's background against the job specs and against each other. Look at the whole person (you will have to live with your choice for a long time).

Making a Job Offer

In most companies, the final offer, including salary, is handled by the HR department. Usually the HR representative discusses directly with the applicant the starting salary, benefits, and other facets of employment. If you're responsible for making the offer in your company, however, it's a good idea to check all the arrangements with your boss and the HR department to avoid misunderstandings.

Finalizing the Salary

Most companies set starting salaries for a job category. You may have a narrow range of flexibility, depending on an applicant's background. But when jobs are difficult to fill, and in many higher-level positions, starting salaries are negotiable. In these types of jobs, an applicant is usually interviewed by several people, and you may have several interviews with finalists before making a decision. Obtain a general idea of each person's salary demands early in this process so that you don't waste time in considering people whose salary requirements are way out of line.

Companies traditionally have used an applicant's salary history as the basis for their offer. Ten or fifteen percent higher than a person's current salary is considered a reasonable offer. Because women usually have been paid less than men, however, basing the salary you offer on current earnings isn't always equitable. If the job had been offered to a man and you would have paid a higher rate based on his salary history, you should offer a woman the same rate, even though her earnings record has been lower. In negotiating salary, keep in mind what you pay currently employed people for doing similar work. Offering a new person considerably more than that amount can cause serious morale problems.

There are exceptions to this rule, of course. Some applicants have capabilities that you believe would be of great value to your company, and to attract these people you may have to pay considerably more than your current top rate. Some companies create special job categories to accommodate this situation. Others pay only what they must and hope that it won't lead to lower morale.

Some companies believe that they can avoid these types of problems by prohibiting their employees from discussing salary. This "code of silence" is virtually impossible to enforce. People talk—and discussion of who makes how much constitutes great gossip. One of my clients gave an employee a significant raise to keep him from leaving. He and the others in the company who were aware of the raise were sworn to secrecy. His boss told me, "That very afternoon our manager in Los Angeles called to ask whether the rumor about this raise was true. Asked where he picked up this information, he said that it was on his e-mail when he got back from lunch." The grapevine in action again!

Salary alone isn't a total compensation package. The total package includes vacations, benefits (such as health insurance and retirement plans), frequency of salary reviews, and incentive programs. Even when the salary you offer is less than an applicant wants, you may persuade that person to take your offer by pointing out how the job will enable him or her to use creativity, engage in work of special interest, and help reach career goals.

The Job Offer

Most companies make job offers orally (no letter and no written agreement). An oral offer is just as binding as a written one. Some companies supplement an oral offer with a letter of confirmation so that there are no misunderstandings about the terms. A job-offer letter should contain these elements:

➤ Title of job (a copy of the job description should be attached)

➤ Starting date

➤ Salary, including an explanation of incentive programs

➤ Benefits (may be in the form of a brochure given to all new employees)

➤ Working hours, location of job, and other working conditions

➤ If pertinent, deadline for acceptance of the offer

Secret Weapon

When you make a job offer, the salary should be stated by pay period—not on an annual basis (specify $1,250 per half-month—not $30,000 per year). Some courts have ruled that if you quote a salary on an annual basis, you're guaranteeing the job for one year.

When the Applicant Is Unsure About Accepting the Job

You've narrowed the field, and your first choice is Hillary. Early in the interview process, you explored her salary requirements, and your offer is in line. At least that's what you thought. Now Hillary demurs. "If I stay where I am, I'll get a raise in a few months that will bring me above that salary. You'll have to do better."

Having received approval of the hire at the salary offered, you have to either reject it, persuade her to take the job by selling her on other advantages, or go back to your boss for approval of the higher rate. What you do depends on many factors. Do you have other viable candidates for the job? If, not, how urgent is it that you fill the job? Determine whether you can legitimately offer other benefits, such as a salary review in six months, opportunity for special training in an area in which she is particularly interested, or other perks. Think over the situation carefully, and discuss it with your manager. *Caution:* Don't make commitments you don't have the authority to honor.

If you and your boss agree that Hillary should still be considered for the position, determine how much above your original offer you're willing to pay and what else you can offer. The meeting with Hillary should take place as soon as possible after you and your manager have determined the maximum deal you can offer. With this in mind, you can negotiate with her and try to reach an acceptable arrangement. Usually, if this new negotiation doesn't lead to agreement, you should discontinue the discussion and seek another candidate. Continuing to haggle over terms of employment is frustrating and keeps you from concentrating on your other duties. You're better off using your time and energy to find another candidate.

Secret Weapon

Don't notify unsuccessful applicants until shortly after your new employee starts work. If the chosen person doesn't start, you can go back to the others without having them feel that they were a second choice.

Countering a Counteroffer

You've knocked yourself out reading résumés, interviewing applicants, and comparing candidates. You make the decision that you'll hire Tom, and he accepts your offer. A week later he calls to tell you that he has changed his mind: When he told his boss that he was leaving, his boss made him a counteroffer.

Frustrating? You bet. To minimize the possibility of a counteroffer, assume that any currently employed candidate will get one. At the time you make your offer, bring it up and make these points:

➤ You know that he has done a great job in his present company. You also realize that when he notifies his company that he's planning to leave, it will undoubtedly make him a counteroffer. Why? Because they need him now.

➤ If his company truly appreciated his work, it wouldn't have waited until he got another job offer to give him a raise. You would have given it to him long ago.

➤ Many people who have accepted counteroffers from a current employer find out that, after the pressure is off, the employer will train or hire someone else and let him go.

➤ He will always be looked on as a disloyal person who threatened to leave just to get more money.

➤ When the time for a raise comes around again, guess whose salary has already been "adjusted"?

When these arguments are used, the number of people who accept counteroffers decreases significantly.

Rejecting the Also-Rans

Some companies just assume that if applicants don't get an offer, they will realize that they were rejected. It's not only courteous but also good business practice to notify the men and women you have interviewed that the job has been filled. You don't have to tell applicants why they didn't get the job. Explanations can lead to misunderstandings and even litigation. The most diplomatic approach is just to state that the background of another candidate was closer to your needs.

Chapter 6

Equal Employment Laws

In This Chapter

➤ The civil rights laws

➤ Legal and illegal questions

➤ Age discrimination

➤ Americans with Disabilities

➤ Sexual harassment

Your efforts to comply with any law aren't as simple as just reading and understanding the statutes. Administrative rulings and various interpretations of the law based on court decisions determine how a law should be applied.

What the Laws Say

The laws governing equal employment affect every aspect of your job as a manager. It begins even before your first contact with an applicant and governs all your relations with employees: how you screen candidates, what you pay employees, how you treat employees on the job—all the way to employees' separation from the company, and sometimes even after that.

Here are the main federal laws that apply to equal employment:

➤ **The Civil Rights Act of 1964**, as amended, prohibits discrimination in employment on the basis of race, color, sex, religion, or national origin. The section of the law that covers employment (Title VII) is the Equal Employment Opportunity (EEO) law and is administered by the Equal Employment Opportunity Commission (EEOC). The EEOC also administers the Age Discrimination in Employment Act (ADEA) and the Americans with Disabilities Act (ADA).

➤ **The Age Discrimination in Employment Act of 1967**, as amended, prohibits discrimination against individuals 40 years of age or older. Some state laws cover all persons over the age of 18.

➤ **The Americans with Disabilities Act of 1990** prohibits discrimination against people who are physically or mentally challenged.

➤ **The Equal Pay Act of 1963** requires that an employee's gender not be considered in determining salary (equal pay for equal work).

Secret Weapon

The interpretation of EEO laws comes from both administrative rulings and court decisions. You should consult an attorney to clarify any actions you take under these laws.

Most states have similar laws. Because some state laws are stricter than the federal laws, make sure that you know what your state requires. In addition, several presidential executive orders require that certain government contractors and other organizations receiving funds from the federal government institute affirmative-action programs to bring more minorities and women into the workplace.

It's important to remember that an employer isn't obligated to hire an applicant just because he or she is in a protected category (such as a person covered by the ADA). An employer can still hire another, better-qualified candidate—it just can't use discriminatory information to *exclude* a candidate who otherwise is most qualified for a job or promotion. Managers must, therefore, avoid doing, asking, or saying anything that could possibly be construed as discriminatory.

What Do You Know About EEO?

To function as a manager today, you must be thoroughly familiar with various state and federal laws concerning equal employment opportunity. To help you measure your knowledge of these laws, take the following quiz. It covers only a few of the key factors in the laws, but should give you some insight into understanding this important area.

Answer Yes or No:

On an application form or in an interview, is it legal to ask:

1. "What are the names of your nearest of kin?" _____

2. "Do you have a permanent immigration visa?" _____

3. "Have you ever been arrested?" _____

Indicate whether each of the following help-wanted ads is legal:

4. "Management trainees: College degree; top 10 percent of class only" _____

continues

continued

5. "Accountant: Part-time opportunity for retiree" _____

6. "Sales: Recent college graduate preferred" _____

Other areas:

7. Companies may give tests to applicants to measure intelligence or personality as long as the publisher of the test guarantees that it is nondiscriminatory. _____

8. A company may refuse to employ applicants because they are over 70. _____

9. A company may refuse to employ an applicant if she is pregnant. _____

10. A company may ask whether a woman has small children at home. _____

A company may indicate an age preference if:

11. It is for a training program. _____

12. Older people cannot qualify for the company pension program. _____

13. The job calls for considerable travel. _____

Miscellaneous questions:

14. A company may specify that it requires a man for a job if the job calls for travel. _____

15. The company may specify that it requires an attractive woman to greet customers and visitors. _____

The following quiz answers are based on federal law, but some states have interpreted the laws somewhat differently. Because new laws, administrative rulings, and judicial interpretations are promulgated from time to time, the reasoning on which these answers are based may change. Keep in mind the job-related-ness of the questions and what kind of effect they have when asked of ethnic minorities. These are key factors in determining the legitimacy of the questions.

1. **No.** You cannot ask about next of kin because the response may show national origin if the name differs from the applicant's. You may not even ask whom to notify in case of emergency until after you hire an applicant.

2. **Yes.** Immigration laws require that aliens working in the United States have a permanent immigration visa (green card).

3. **No.** Courts have ruled that because some minorities are more likely than nonminorities to be arrested for minor offenses, asking about an arrest record is discriminatory. You *can* ask about convictions for felonies.

4. **No.** Unless you can substantiate that students from the top ten percent of their class have performed significantly better than students with lower grades, this ad isn't job-related.

5. **No.** Because most retirees are over the age of 60, specifying a "retiree" implies that persons between the ages of 40 and 60 are not welcome. The Age Discrimination in Employment Act protects all persons older than 40 against discrimination because of their age.

6. **No.** The phrase "recent college graduate" implies youth. Even the implication of "youth" violates the terms of the ADEA.

7. **No.** The Supreme Court, in *Griggs vs. Duke Power Co.*, upheld the EEOC's requirement that intelligence and personality tests must have a direct relationship to effectiveness on the job for the specific job for which the test is used. Because only the company using the test can verify this relationship, it must be validated against each company's experience.

8. **No.** The Age Discrimination in Employment Act as amended prohibits discrimination against people who are 40 years or older. There is no top age limit.

9. **No.** Pregnant women may not be refused employment unless the work might endanger their health (such as heavy physical work or exposure to dangerous substances). Employers cannot ask an applicant whether she is pregnant or comment that the company doesn't hire pregnant women. If a pregnant woman were rejected, the company would have to prove that the reason for the rejection was a factor other than her pregnancy.

10. **No.** Because men aren't usually asked whether they have small children at home, it has been interpreted as a means of discriminating against women.

11. **No.** Training programs may not be limited to young people.

12. **No.** Participation in a pension program is not an acceptable reason for age discrimination.

13. **No.** Ability to travel is not related to age.

14. **No.** Ability to travel is not related to gender.

15. **No.** A company's desire to have an attractive woman as a receptionist doesn't make it a bona fide occupational qualification.

Every manager who hires people should, ideally, score 100 percent on this quiz. Failure to comply with any one of these rules may result in complaints, investigations, hearings, and penalties.

Bona Fide Occupational Qualifications (BFOQs)

There are some positions for which a company is permitted to specify only a man or only a woman for the job. Clear-cut reasons must exist, however, for why a person of only that gender can perform the job. In the law, these reasons are referred to as *bona fide occupational qualifications,* or *BFOQs.*

If a job calls for heavy lifting, for example, is it a BFOQ for men only? Not necessarily. There are strong women who are able to do the job, and there are weak men who cannot. It's legitimate to require that all applicants—both men and women—pass a weight-lifting test.

And that's not all. Suppose that a job calls for driving a forklift truck and that the operator is occasionally required to do heavy lifting. A woman applicant may be able to drive the truck but not be able to do the lifting. If the lifting is only a small part of the job, you cannot reject her. She is capable of performing the major aspect of the work, and other people can be assigned to handle the lifting.

Meanings and Gleanings

The only undisputed *bona fide occupational qualifications* are a wet nurse (for a woman) and a sperm donor (for a man).

Lawful and Unlawful Questions

The "lawful and unlawful" questions in the following table are presented as general guidelines that apply under federal laws and the laws of the strictest states. To ensure that you're in compliance with legal requirements and interpretations in any specific state, however, check with local authorities and an attorney specializing in this field.

Note: Questions that would otherwise be deemed lawful may in certain circumstances be deemed as evidence of unlawful discrimination when the question seeks to elicit information about a selection criterion that isn't job-related, has a disproportionate effect on the members of a minority group, and cannot be justified by business necessity.

Lawful and Unlawful Pre-Employment Questions

Subject	Lawful	Unlawful
Age	"Are you 18 years or older? If not, state age."	"How old are you?" "What is your date of birth?" "What year did you graduate?"
Arrest Record	"Have you ever been convicted of a crime? (Give details.)"	"Have you ever been arrested?"
Birth control	None.	Inquiry into capacity to reproduce or advocacy of any form of birth control or family planning.
Birthdate	None. (After person is employed, proof of age for insurance or other purpose may be requested.)	Requirements that applicant submit birth certificate, naturalization, or baptismal record.
		Requirement that applicant produce proof of age in the form of a birth certificate or baptismal record.

Subject	Lawful	Unlawful
Birthplace	None.	Birthplace of applicant. Birthplace of applicant's parents, spouse, or other close relatives.
Citizenship	"Are you a citizen of the United States? If not a citizen of the United States, do you intend to become a citizen of the United States? If not a citizen of the United States, have you the legal right to remain permanently in the United States?"	"Of what country are you a citizen?" "Do you intend to remain permanently in the United States?" Whether applicant is naturalized or native-born citizen. "On what date did you acquire citizenship?" Requirement that applicant produce naturalization papers or first papers. "Are your parents or spouse naturalized or native-born citizens of the United States?" "On what date did your parents or spouse acquire citizenship?"

continues

continued

Subject	Lawful	Unlawful
Disability	"Do you have any impairments (physical, mental, or medical) that would interfere with your ability to perform the job for which you have applied?"	"Do you have a disability?" "Have you ever been treated for any of the following diseases?" (followed by list of diseases)
Driver's License	"Do you possess a valid driver's license?"	Requirement that applicant produce a driver's license prior to employment.
Education	Inquiry into applicant's academic, vocational, or professional education and schools attended.	None.
Experience	Inquiry into work experience.	None.
Gender	None.	Any inquiry about gender on application form or interview. "Do you wish to be addressed as Mr., Miss, Mrs., or Ms.?"

Subject	Lawful	Unlawful
Language	Inquiry into languages applicant speaks and writes fluently.	"What is your native language?" or any inquiry into how applicant acquired ability to read, write, or speak a foreign language.
Marital Status	None.	"Are you married, single, divorced, or separated?" Name or other information about spouse. Where spouse works. "How many children do you have?" "How old are your children?" "What arrangements have you made for child care when you're at work?"
Military Experience	Inquiry into applicant's military experience in the Armed Forces of the United States or in a state militia. Inquiry into applicant's service in a specific branch of United States Armed Forces.	Inquiry into applicant's general military experience (for example, a military unit of another country).

continues

continued

Subject	Lawful	Unlawful
Name	"Have you ever worked for this company under a different name?"	Original name of applicant whose name has been changed by court order or otherwise. Maiden name of married woman.
	"Is any additional information (a change of name or use of assumed name or nickname) necessary to enable a check of your work record? If yes, explain."	"Have you have ever worked under a different name? State name and dates."
National Origin	None.	Inquiry into applicant's lineage, ancestry, national origin, descent, parentage, or nationality. Spouse's nationality. "What is your native tongue?"
Notify in Case of Emergency	None.	Name and address of person to be notified in case of an emergency. (This information may be asked only after an applicant is employed.)

Subject	Lawful	Unlawful
Organizations	Inquiry into applicant's memberships in organizations that the applicant considers relevant to his ability to perform the job.	"List all clubs, societies, and lodges to which you belong."
Photograph	None.	Requirement or option that applicant affix a photograph to employment form at any time before being hired.
Race or Color	None.	Complexion, color of skin, coloring.
Relatives	Names of applicant's relatives other than spouse already employed by company.	Names, addresses, number, or other information concerning applicant's spouse, children, or other relatives not employed by the company.
Religion or Creed	None.	Inquiry into applicant's religious denomination, religious affiliations, church, parish, pastor, or religious holidays observed. Applicants may not be told "This is a Catholic (or Protestant or Jewish) organization."

Age Discrimination

Despite federal and state laws, the accent on youth in many companies has kept productive men and women from getting and keeping jobs or from functioning at their highest levels in a job. Study after study has shown that mature people are at least as productive and creative as their younger counterparts are, and that they are more reliable and make better judgments and decisions than their younger counterparts.

Avoiding Age Discrimination in Hiring

Even though most company application forms don't ask a person's age or date of birth and most people omit that information from their résumés, it's still easy to guess an applicant's age range within a few years. A team leader who prefers that young people join his or her team may overlook, just because of age, potential members who could be of great value to the team.

The Americans with Disabilities Act (ADA)

The newest and probably least understood civil rights law is the Americans with Disabilities Act (ADA). Your company must adhere to this law if it has 15 or more employees. The ADA makes it illegal to discriminate in hiring, in job assignments, and in the treatment of employees because of a disability. Employers must make *reasonable accommodation* so that these people can perform the essential duties of their jobs.

This accommodation can vary from building access ramps for wheelchair users to providing special equipment for people who are seeing- or hearing-challenged. Such accommodation is required unless this type of accommodation is an *undue hardship* for the company. Undue hardship is usually defined in monetary terms. If an applicant who uses a wheelchair applies for a job with a small company, the cost of building an elevator or a ramp to give access to the floor on which the job is located may be a financial hardship. Because of this undue hardship, the company could reject the applicant or provide a less expensive accommodation if possible. If the same applicant applied for a job in a more affluent company, however, it might not be considered undue hardship to do the necessary construction.

Secret Weapon

In the decision to select or promote someone, don't focus on disabilities. Concentrate on that person's *abilities*.

Sexual Harassment

Organizations of all sizes and types have faced charges brought against them by both female and male employees who claim sexual harassment by managers at all levels, and even by nonmanagerial employees. The courts and the EEOC define sexual harassment as any unwelcome sexual advances or requests for sexual favors or any conduct of a sexual nature when:

➤ Submission is made explicitly or implicitly a condition of initial or continued employment.

➤ Submission or rejection is used as a basis of working conditions including promotion, salary adjustment, assignment of work, or termination.

➤ Such conduct has the purpose or effect of substantially interfering with an individual's work environment or creates an intimidating, hostile, or offensive work environment.

Some men (and a few women) in positions of authority make it clear to subordinates that if they want to get favorable treatment or even keep their jobs, they must submit to these demands. But the harassment is often much more subtle. They don't make any actual demands; instead, they imply them. They make references to other employees who have benefited by being "more friendly" or they comment about a person's physical attributes.

"Wait a minute," you say. "If I tell a woman that she's attractive, *that's* harassment?" It depends on what you say and how you say it. The comment "That's an attractive dress" is much different from the comment "That dress is sexy." The statement "I like your new hairdo" is acceptable, but the statement "Wearing your hair like that excites me" is not.

What Is an Intimidating, Hostile Work Environment?

Sexual harassment isn't limited to demands for sexual favors: It also includes conduct that creates an intimidating and hostile work environment.

Ken's team has always been all male, and now two women have been added to his group. Some of the men resent this "intrusion" on their masculine camaraderie and make life unpleasant for the female team members. The men make snide remarks, give the women incorrect information that causes them to make errors in their work, and exclude them from work-related discussions. No actions are taken that can be interpreted as "sexual" in nature, but it still qualifies as sexual harassment. The men have created a hostile work environment for the women.

If you're faced with a similar situation, talk to the people (or person) using the inappropriate language. Point out diplomatically that their behavior is unprofessional and offensive to both women and men and that it isn't appropriate to use it in a business environment. Inform them that such behavior can cause legal problems for them and the company. Tell them that if they continue to use street language they will be subject to disciplinary action.

Secret Weapon

Companies can protect themselves from charges of sexual harassment by establishing and publicizing a procedure for dealing with complaints—and all complaints, if true, should be quickly investigated and corrected.

Ten Steps to Protect Your Company from Sexual Harassment Charges

1. Establish a formal policy prohibiting sexual harassment. Clearly indicate all actions that could be construed as harassment and what steps employees should take if they are harassed. Appoint a senior executive to administer the policy.

2. Publicize the policy through bulletins, articles in the company newspaper, regularly scheduled meetings, and training programs.

3. Make it easy for complainants to bring matters to the attention of management. Post notices throughout your offices detailing to whom and how employees should bring up their complaints.

4. Investigate all complaints—no matter how trivial or unjustified they appear to you. Keep written records of all findings (including memos, reports of interviews, and statements from the complainant, the person accused, and witnesses).

5. Never terminate or threaten complainants or potential complainants.

6. Don't make rash decisions. Analyze all the facts. Consult your attorney (remember, it may wind up in court).

7. Take action. If the complaint is justified, correct the situation. Depending on the case, this may include requiring the harasser to apologize, ordering a cessation of the acts that led to the complaint, adjusting the salary, promoting or changing the working conditions of the persons who have suffered, or, in flagrant or repeated offenses, firing the harasser.

8. If the investigation finds the complaint was not justified, explain the decision carefully and diplomatically to the complainant. Keep in mind that if he or she is not satisfied, a charge can still be filed with appropriate government agencies or brought to court.

9. Don't look for easy ways out. Transferring the harasser to another department may solve the immediate problem, but if the harasser repeats the offense in the new assignment, the situation is compounded.

10. If a formal complaint is made to the EEOC or a state equivalent—even if you feel the complaint is groundless—treat it seriously.

Twelve Ways to Keep Alert to Your EEO Responsibility

Go along with the spirit as well as the letter of the law.

Offer women and minorities opportunities that were previously denied to them.

Open training programs to minorities, women, and the physically challenged, and encourage them, by offering counseling and support, to complete these programs.

Discipline should be administered equitably and should be carefully documented.

Be aware of your own biases and work to overcome any influence they may have on your job decisions.

Use everyone's abilities optimally. Don't base your views about a person's abilities on age, sex, or race. Judge people not on what they cannot do, but on what they *can* do.

Set realistic performance standards based on what a job really calls for. Do not specify, for example, that a job calls for heavy lifting when most of the lifting is done mechanically.

Ignore stereotypes and judge people by their individual abilities, strengths, and weaknesses.

Never use racial epithets or slurs—even in jest.

Encourage all people to deal with all their coworkers as human beings. Mold them into a team.

Sex life and job life must be kept separate.

Support your company's equal-employment and affirmative-action programs fully in every aspect of your job.

Follow these suggestions. They add up to **Good Business.**

Chapter 7

Communicating

In This Chapter

➤ Getting your ideas across to others

➤ Understanding why people may not understand you

➤ Being a better listener

These days, communication—what you say and how you say it—can determine whether you succeed or fail. This skill, shared by most successful professionals, business executives, and government leaders, is a skill you, too, can acquire. All you need is the will to improve and the determination. Once you've improved your ability to communicate, you can present your ideas more effectively to your boss, your peers, your associates, your customers, your team, even your friends and family.

What You Say

Suppose that you call a team meeting to discuss a new project. Or you sit down with an associate for a serious discussion about performance. Or perhaps you're called upon to present a progress report to the executive committee. In all these situations, *communication*—your choice of words and your delivery of them—may make the difference between your success or failure.

Whether you're addressing a group or having a one-to-one conversation, you should think out your message and how you plan to present it in advance. Sometimes you'll have to think on your feet with little or no time to prepare, but more often than not, when you're required to discuss something, you *can* prepare on short notice.

Meanings and Gleanings

Communication takes place when persons or groups exchange information, ideas, and concepts.

Know Your Subject

On the job, you'll usually communicate with others about subjects you're thoroughly familiar with: the work you're doing, matters in your own area of expertise, or company-related problems. Still, you should review the facts to be sure that you have a handle on all the available information and are prepared to answer any questions.

From time to time, you may be asked to report on matters with which you are unfamiliar. Your company may want to purchase a new type of computer software, for example, and ask you to check it out. Here's how you should start tackling the assignment:

➤ Learn as much as possible about the subject.

➤ Know ten times more than you'll likely need to know for the presentation.

➤ Prepare notes about the pluses and minuses of the proposed purchase, solution, and so on.

➤ Whether you will make this report to one person (your boss, for example) or to a group of managers or technical specialists, be prepared to answer questions about any subject that might come up.

Know Your Audience

Even the most skilled orator will fail to communicate effectively if his audience can't understand him. Half of good communication is understanding your audience. Choose words that your listeners will easily comprehend. If the people you're addressing all come from a technical background, you can use technical terminology. Your listeners will clearly and readily understand these special terms. But if you talk about technical subject matter to an audience unfamiliar with it, drop the technical language. If your listeners can't understand your vocabulary, your message will be lost.

Secret Weapon

Don't use jargon—those special initials, acronyms, and words that are used only in your field or in just your company—when communicating with those not in the know.

How You Say It

No matter how well-thought-out your message is, no one will understand it unless you express it clearly and distinctly. Here are some common problems people have with speaking clearly:

➤ **Mumbling.** Swallowing word endings. Speaking with your mouth almost closed. Practice in front of a mirror. Open up those lips.

➤ **Speaking too fast.** Whoa! Give people a chance to absorb what you're saying.

➤ **Speaking too slowly.** Speak too slowly, and you'll lose your audience. While you're plodding through your message, their minds wander to other matters.

➤ **Mispronouncing words.** Not sure how a word is pronounced? Look it up or ask someone who does know.

➤ **Speaking in a monotone.** Vary the inflection, tone, and pitch of your voice. Otherwise, you'll put your listeners to sleep.

Listen to Your Own Voice

You don't hear yourself as others hear you. Get a voice-activated tape recorder, place it on your desk, and record your voice when you talk to others in person or on the phone. Listen to yourself on tape. The recording will tell you whether you mumble, speak too fast (or perhaps too slowly), or speak in a monotone.

Secret Weapon

When you leave a message on voice mail, listen to it before you hang up. By listening to yourself, you'll hear how you sound to others.

Add Video to the Audio

People remember much more of what they see than what they hear, and they remember even more of what they see and hear simultaneously. If people *see* something when you present your message (that is, if you use visual aids), it makes your message that much clearer, more exciting, and, most important, more memorable. Here are some suggestions that will give an added dimension to your talk:

➤ Use graphs or charts to clarify figures.

➤ Use photos, drawings, or diagrams to illustrate points.

➤ Use flowcharts to describe processes.

The following visual effects are available for you to use in presentations to a group:

➤ **Flip charts and chalkboards.** The least-expensive and easiest items to use.

➤ **Overhead projectors.** Can be used to display prepared transparencies, which you can refer to and augment as you talk.

➤ **Slide presentations.** Colorful and dramatic slides can bring out important points.

➤ **Videos or films.** A much more expensive aid, but worth it, particularly if your presentation will be repeated several times.

Are You Listening?

Suppose that one of your colleagues brings a problem to you and asks for help. You begin listening attentively, but before you know it, your mind is wandering. Instead of listening to the problem, you're thinking about the pile of work on your desk, the meeting you have scheduled with the company vice president, or the scuffle your son got into at school.

Does this happen to you? Of course it does. It happens to all of us. Our minds can process ideas ten times faster than we can talk. While someone is talking, your mind may race ahead. You complete the speaker's sentence in your mind—often incorrectly—long before he or she does.

You "hear" what your mind dictates, not what's actually said. This is human nature. But that's no excuse for being a bad listener. Read on to learn how to listen more effectively.

"I Wasn't Listening"

Now suppose that your mind was wandering and that you didn't hear what the other person said. It's embarrassing to admit that you weren't listening, so you fake it. You pick up on the last few words you heard and comment on them. If you make sense, you're lucky. But you may have missed the real gist of the discussion.

When you haven't been listening, you don't have to admit, "I'm sorry, I was daydreaming." One way to get back on track is to ask a question or make a comment about the last item you did hear: "Can we go back a minute to such-and-such?" Another method is to comment this way: "To make sure that I can better understand your view on this, please elaborate."

Secret Weapon

When you realize that you haven't been paying full attention—when the words begin to be replaced by a droning sound, when you hear words but not ideas, or when you guess what you *think* will be said—Stop! Start listening!

Five Tricks to Make You a Better Listener

You *can* become a better listener. You can stop some of the main causes of ineffective listening before they begin. All you have to do is make a few changes in your work environment and in your approach to listening—a small effort with a big return.

1. **Eliminate distractions.** The greatest distraction is probably the telephone. You want to give the speaker your full attention—*and the phone rings.* Answering the call not only interrupts your discussion, but also disrupts the flow of your thoughts. Even after you've hung up, your mind may still be pondering the call.

   If you know that you'll be having a lengthy discussion at your desk, arrange for someone else to handle your calls or set your voice mail to pick up all calls right away. If this isn't possible, get away from the telephone. Try an empty conference room. Of course, there's probably a phone in the conference room, but no one knows that you're there, so it probably won't ring.

2. **Get rid of excess paper to reduce distractions.** If your desk is strewn with paper, you'll probably end up skimming them and realize too late that you're reading a letter or memo instead of listening. Put those papers away in a drawer. Or go to a conference room and take only the papers that are related to your discussion.

3. **Don't get too comfortable.** Some years ago I was discussing a situation with another manager. As was my custom, I sat in my comfortable executive chair with my hands behind my head. Maybe I rocked a little. Fortunately, I caught myself before I dozed off. Ever since then, I've made a point of sitting on the edge of my chair and leaning forward rather than backward when I engage in discussions. This position not only brings me physically closer to the other person, but also enables me to be more attentive and helps me to maintain eye contact. It also shows the other person that I'm truly interested in

getting the full story he or she is relating and that I take seriously what is being said. And because I'm not quite so comfortable, I have less of a tendency to daydream.

4. **Be an active listener.** An *active listener* doesn't just sit or stand back with open ears. An active listener asks questions about what's being said. You can paraphrase ("So the way I understand it is that...") or ask specific questions about specific points. This technique not only enables you to clarify points that may be unclear but also keeps you alert so that you can give the speaker your full attention.

Meanings and Gleanings

An *active listener* not only pays close attention to what the other party says, but asks questions, makes comments, and reacts verbally and nonverbally to what is said.

5. **Be an empathetic listener.** Listen with your heart as well as with your head. Empathetic listeners not only listen to what other people say, but also try to feel what other people are feeling when they say it.

Take Notes

It's impossible to remember everything that's said in a lengthy discussion. Jot down key words or phrases. Write down figures or important facts—just enough to remind you of the principal points that were made. If you're concentrating on what you're writing, you can't pay full attention to the conversation. Immediately after a meeting, while the information is still fresh in your mind, write a detailed summary.

Body Language

People communicate not only through words, but also through their gestures, facial expressions, and movements. Wouldn't it be great if you could buy a dictionary of body language? Then you could easily interpret non-verbal language.

Secret Weapon

Make a conscious effort to study and remember people's individual body language.

Unfortunately, no such dictionary could exist because body language isn't standardized like verbal language. Body language differs from one person to another. When people nod as you speak, for example, you might assume that they're agreeing with you. However, some people nod just to acknowledge that they're listening. When someone folds his arms as you speak, you might think his action is a subconscious show of disagreement. But it could simply be that your listener is just cold!

What You Send Might Not Be What's Received

Communication works like a two-way radio: two parties sending messages and responding to each other. Sometimes, however, the message that's received may not be exactly the same as the message that was sent. Somewhere between the sender's radio and the receiver's radio, static may have intervened and distorted the message. This static may be generated from either end of the connection.

What causes the static in direct conversations? It might be rooted in your own mind. Everything you say and hear is filtered through your brain and influenced by the attitudes you've acquired over the years. The following points detail some of those attitudes:

➤ **Assumptions.** You've seen this situation repeatedly. For example, you have a pretty good idea about what causes a particular problem and how to solve it. In discussing it with others, you assume that they know as much about it as you do, and you give instructions based on the assumption that they have know-how, although they may not. The result is that you don't give them adequate information.

➤ **Preconceptions.** People tend to hear what they expect to hear. The message you receive is distorted by any material information you have already have heard about the subject. So if the new information is different from what's expected, you might reject it as being incorrect.

What does this mean to you? Keep your mind open. When someone tells you something, make an extra effort to listen and to evaluate the new information objectively instead of blocking it out because it differs from your preconceptions.

Meetings and Conferences

In addition to team or department-level meetings, managers often participate in company-wide conferences or conventions. A relatively recent innovation in company communications is the retreat. A group of managers is invited to a facility away from the company offices—usually a resort hotel—to relax and informally discuss company problems. You'll play golf or tennis, take nature walks, go canoeing, build campfires, or splurge on buffets. The hope is that staff members will loosen up and be more creative in presenting ideas and more receptive to receiving them.

If you are invited, of course, you should accept—it's less of an invitation than a command. Sure, have fun. Participate in the discussions. But prepare what you will say and be businesslike in your demeanor. Dress informally, but not loudly. Drink moderately. Watch what you say.

On the positive side, you may get to know your boss better, or make contacts with people in other departments or from different locations in the company, which can be very valuable in getting your work done and advancing your career

Secret Weapon

When attending a convention or retreat, don't relax completely. Everything you do and say will be noticed. Don't gripe or complain. The other participants are not necessarily your buddies. They may be your bosses or your rivals for advancement, recognition, or power.

Getting the Most from Conferences

Most managers who attend conferences often complain that they get few benefits from them. Here are ten steps that will help make such meetings more meaningful to you:

1. **Plan and prepare.** Most conferences are announced months in advance. Usually an agenda accompanies the announcement. Study it carefully. Does any subject listed require special preparation? You may want to read a book or an article on unfamiliar subjects to help you comprehend and contribute to the discussion. You may want to reexamine your company's

experience in that area so that you can relate what is being discussed to your own problems.

2. **Don't sit with your colleagues.** You can speak to them anytime. Here is your chance to meet new people. At many meetings, participants are seated at tables either for the entire program or for parts of it. Make a point of sitting with different people at various stages of the meetings. Especially at luncheon or dinner discussions, you can often pick up more ideas from your tablemates than from the speakers. In addition, you can make new contacts who may be valuable resources for information after the conference ends.

3. **Open your mind.** You go to conferences and conventions to learn. To get the most out of what a speaker says, keep your mind open to new suggestions. They may be different from what you honestly believe is best, but until you hear it all and think it through objectively, you don't really know. Progress comes through change. This does not mean that all new ideas are good ones, but they should be listened to, evaluated, and carefully and objectively considered.

4. **Be tolerant.** Have you ever listened to a speaker who turned you off immediately? You didn't like his or her appearance, clothes, voice, or regional accent so you either stopped listening or rejected what he or she said. Prejudice against a speaker keeps many an attendee from really listening to what is discussed or from accepting the ideas presented.

During a conference break, I overheard one participant tell another: "This meeting is a waste of time. How can a woman tell us men how to market machine tools? She ought to stick to housewares or cosmetics." Sexist prejudice prevented him from acquiring valuable information, which could have been important to his company.

5. **Take notes.** Note-taking has two important functions. It helps organize what you hear while you are at the conference, which leads to more systematic listening. It also becomes a source for future reference.

6. **Ask questions.** Don't hesitate to query a speaker when the opportunity arises. But don't waste other people's time with trivial questions.

7. **Contribute ideas.** Some people will always contribute more than others; some just sit and listen. When asked why they didn't participate more fully, they say: "Why should I give my ideas to these people? Some of them are my competitors and I won't give away my trade secrets."

Nobody expects you to say anything that would damage your firm or its competitive position, but most discussions are not of this nature. They're designed instead to promote the exchange of general ideas. The experience of one organization helps the others. By contributing ideas, you provide richer experiences for everyone else, which in turn results in a more fulfilling experience for you.

Secret Weapon

Keep a record of the names and addresses of the speakers you hear. You may want to contact some of them for additional information. Record names and addresses of people you meet. They may be a source of information in the future.

8. **Summarize.** After the meeting, review your notes while the meeting is still fresh in your mind. Write or dictate a report on the conference for your permanent files.

9. **Report.** Report on what you have learned to your boss or others in your organization, who might find the information valuable. By sharing what you have learned, you add to the value your firm receives from sending you to the convention.

10. **Apply what you have learned.** If you don't do anything with what you learned at the conference, it has been a waste of time and money.

Chapter 8

Motivating

In This Chapter

➤ Getting to know your team members

➤ Recognizing your team as a motivational force

➤ Money and benefits: motivators or satisfiers?

➤ Praise and recognition

Look at the word *motivation*. Two other words that begin with the same three letters are *motion* and *motor*. We call the motors in our cars "internal combustion engines," and each of us has inside us a combustion engine that's keeping us in motion. As a team leader, your job is to provide each of your team members with the fuel that will start their "motors" and keep them going. Of course, not all motors take the same kind of fuel to keep them running; and so it is with people. What motivates one person may not work for another. To be able to help your team move forward, you have to know what kind of fuel to feed to each of your members, how and when to use it, and what reaction you can expect. Tough job? Sure, but it's worth the effort.

As team leader, you should meld your team members into a cohesive group and work with them to develop within themselves that motivation that will propel them toward accomplishing the team's goals.

Motivating for Peak Performance

Your first job as a team leader is to develop the skills and abilities of each of your associates so that they can perform at top capacity. The best way to begin is to learn about each person as an individual. Maybe you think that all you really have to know about your associates is how well they do their work. Wrong! Knowing the members of your team requires more than just knowing their job skills. Learn what's important to your team members— their ambitions and goals, their families, their special concerns—in other words, what makes them tick.

Secret Weapon

"Good management consists of inspiring average people to do the work of superior people."

—John D. Rockefeller

Method of Operation

If you've ever watched crime shows or read detective novels, you know about the term *M.O.* (*modus operandi,* or method of operation). Detectives often can tell who has committed a crime by his or her M.O.—the manner in which the crime was committed—because criminals tend to repeat the same M.O.s in all of their crimes.

Meanings and Gleanings

A person's *M.O.* is the method, or mode, of operation—
the pattern of behavior that a person habitually follows in
performing works.

We all have M.O.s in the way we do our work and the way
we live our lives. Study the way each of your team members
operates, and you'll discover his or her M.O. For example,
you might notice that one team member always ponders a
subject before commenting on it, and another might reread
everything she's worked on several times before starting
new work. Psychologists don't call them M.O.s; they call
them "patterns of behavior." Whatever you call M.O.s, being aware of them helps you understand people and enables you to work with them more effectively.

By observing and listening, you can learn a great deal
about your colleagues. Listen when they speak to you: Listen to what they say, and listen to what they *don't* say.
Listen when they speak to others. Eavesdropping may not
be polite, but you can learn a great deal. Observe how
your team members do their work and how they act and
react. It doesn't take long to identify their likes and dis-
likes, their quirks and eccentricities. By listening, you can
learn about the things that are important to each of them
and the "hot buttons" that can turn them on or off.

Getting to Know Your Team Members
By observing and listening, you might realize that Claudia
is a creative person. If you want to excite her about her
role in an assignment, you can do so by appealing to her

creativity. You notice that Mike is slow when he's learning
new things, but that after he learns them he works quickly
and accurately. To enable Mike to do his best, you know
that you'll need patience. It helps to keep an informal reminder of each of your team members' traits.

Secret Weapon

Encourage your associates to express their ideas, especially
when they differ from yours. Their disagreements not only
provide you with new ideas, but also give you insight into
their M.O.s.

Money as a Motivator

Here's a mini-lesson in logic:

> A: The more money you earn, the happier you are.
>
> B: The more work you produce, the more money
> you earn.
>
> Therefore:
>
> C: People will stretch to produce more so that they
> can become happier.

But is it true? Sometimes, but not always. Assume A and B
are both true; it should logically follow that C is true.
Right? Sometimes it is, but often it is not. Let's look into
why money is not always the motivator that it logically
appears to be.

Motivators Versus Satisfiers

A team of behavioral scientists led by Frederick Herzberg
studied what people want from their jobs and classified
the results into two categories:

1. **Satisfiers (also called maintenance factors).** Factors people require from a job to justify minimum effort. These factors include working conditions, money, and benefits. After employees are satisfied, however, just giving them more of the same factors doesn't *motivate* them to work harder. Many of what most people consider motivators are really just satisfiers.

2. **Motivators.** Factors that stimulate people to put out more energy, effort, and enthusiasm in their job.

Suppose that you work in a less-than-adequate facility, in which lighting is poor, ventilation is inadequate, and space is tight. Productivity, of course, is low. In a few months, your company moves to new quarters with excellent lighting and air-conditioning and lots of space, and productivity shoots up.

The company CEO is elated. He says to the board of directors, "I've found the solution to high productivity: If you give people better working conditions, they'll produce more, so I'm going to make the working conditions even better." He hires an interior designer, has new carpet installed, hangs paintings on the walls, and places plants around the office. The employees are delighted. It's a pleasure to work in these surroundings—but productivity doesn't increase at all.

Meanings and Gleanings

When managers *motivate*, they stimulate people to exert more effort, energy, and enthusiasm. The best motivation is self-motivation. Provide a climate in which self-motivation flourishes.

Why not? People seek a level of satisfaction in their job—in this case, reasonably good working conditions. When the working environment was made acceptable, employees were satisfied, and it showed up in their productivity. After the conditions met their level of satisfaction, however, adding enhancements didn't motivate them.

So What Does This Have to Do with Money?

Money, like working conditions, is a satisfier. You might assume that offering more money generates higher productivity. And you're probably right—for most people, but not for everyone. Incentive programs, in which people are given an opportunity to earn more money by producing more, are a part of many company compensation plans. They work for some people, but not for others.

The sales department is a good example. Because salespeople usually work on a commission, or incentive, basis, they're in the enviable position of rarely having to ask for a raise. If salespeople want to earn more money, all they have to do is work harder or smarter and make as much money as they want. Therefore, all salespeople are very rich. Right? Wrong! How come this logic doesn't work? Sales managers have complained about this problem from the beginning of time. They say, "We have an excellent incentive program, and the money is there for our sales staff. All they have to do is reach out—and they don't. Why not?"

You have to delve deep into the human psyche for an answer. We all set personal salary levels, consciously or subconsciously, at which we are satisfied. Until we reach that point, money does motivate us, but after that—no more. *This level varies significantly from person to person.* Some people set this point very high, and money is a major motivator to them; others are content at lower levels. It doesn't mean that they don't want their annual raise or bonus, but if obtaining the extra money requires special effort or inconvenience, you can forget it.

Secret Weapon

Even if you have no control over basic satisfiers—working conditions, salary, benefits, and the like—as a supervisor, you have the opportunity to use the real motivators: job satisfaction, recognition, and achievement.

Suppose that Derek is in your production group and that his salary is 60 percent of yours. His wife works, but you know by the nature of her job that it doesn't pay much. Derek drives a twelve-year-old car and buys his clothes from thrift shops. The only vacations his family has ever taken are occasional camping trips. You feel sorry for him. But now you can help Derek: You need several workers for a special project to be done over the next six Saturdays at double-time pay. When you ask Derek whether he wants the assignment, he says "No," and you can't understand why. It seems to you that he should be eager to make more money, but he has already reached his level of satis-faction. To him, having the Saturday off to be with his family is more important than the opportunity to earn more money.

This example doesn't mean that money doesn't motivate at all. The opportunity to earn money motivates everyone to the point that they are satisfied. Some people, like Derek, are content at lower levels. As long as they can meet their basic needs, other things are more important to them than money. To other people, this point is very high, and they "knock themselves out" to keep making more money.

By learning as much as you can about your associates, you learn about their interests, goals, and lifestyles and the level of income at which they're satisfied. To offer the opportunity to make more money as an incentive to people who don't care about it is futile. You have to find some other ways to motivate them.

Benefits: Motivators or Satisfiers?

Most companies provide some form of health insurance, life insurance, pensions, and other benefits to their employees. In fact, the benefits package is one of the factors that potential employees seek when they evaluate a job offer—but it isn't a motivator. (Have you ever known anyone who worked harder because the company introduced a dental insurance program?) Benefits are satisfiers. Good benefits attract people to work for a company, and they also keep people from quitting. (Sometimes, the people you wish would quit don't.)

Secret Weapon

Keeping employees happy is not enough. The challenge is to develop high performance standards that challenge employees and motivate them to stretch to meet those standards.

Recognition

Human beings crave recognition. People like to know that others know who they are, what they want, and what they believe. Recognition begins when you learn and use people's names. Of course you know the names of the men and women on your team, but you will be coordinating work with other teams, with internal and external suppliers, subcontractors, and customers. Everyone has a name. Learn it. Use it. It's your first step in recognizing each person's individuality.

In Woody's exit interview after quitting his job with the Building Maintenance Company, he was asked what he liked most and least about the company. Woody responded that, although the salary and benefits were good, he never felt that he was part of the organization. "I always felt that I was looked at as nothing more than a cog in the machine," he said. "During the nine months I worked in the department, I made several suggestions, offered to take on extra projects, and tried to apply creative approaches to some of the work assigned to me. My boss didn't recognize all that I could have contributed."

Show You Care

Just as you have a life outside the company, so does every member of your team. A job is an important part of our lives, but there are many aspects of life that may be of greater importance: health, family, and outside interests, for example. Show sincere interest in a team member's total person.

Virginia, the head teller of a savings-and-loan association in Wichita, Kansas, makes a point of welcoming back associates who have been on vacation or out for several days because of illness. She asks them about their vacation or the state of their health and brings them up-to-date on company news. She makes them feel that she missed them—and it comes across sincerely because she really did miss them.

Jacob, a grandfather, realizes that children are the center of most families. He takes a genuine interest in the activities of his coworkers' children and has even accompanied

associates to school events in which their children participate. Some people may consider this situation paternalis-
tic or intrusive, but Jake's true concern comes across as
positive interest and has helped meld his team members
into a "working family."

Secret Weapon

People need praise. If employees do nothing that merits
praise, assign them projects in which they can demonstrate
success and then praise their accomplishments.

Five Tips for Effective Praise

As important as praise is in motivating people, it doesn't
always work. Some supervisors praise every minor activity,
diminishing the value of praise for real accomplishments.
Others deliver praise in such a way that it seems phony.
To make your praise more meaningful, follow these suggestions:

1. **Don't overdo it.** Praise is sweet. Candy is sweet, too,
   but the more you eat, the less sweet each piece becomes—and you may get a stomachache. Too much
   praise reduces the benefit that's derived from each
   bit of praise; if it's overdone, it loses its value alto-
   gether.

2. **Be sincere.** You can't fake sincerity. You must truly
   believe that what you're praising your associate for
   is actually commendable. If you don't believe it
   yourself, neither will your associate.

3. **Be specific about the reason for your praise.**
   Rather than say, "Great job!" it's much better to say,

"The report you submitted on the XYZ matter enabled me to understand more clearly the complexities of the issue."

4. **Ask for your team members' advice.** Nothing is more flattering than to be asked for advice about how to handle a situation. This approach can backfire, though, if you don't *take* the advice. If you have to reject advice, ask people questions about their inadequate answers until *they* see the error of their ways and reissue good advice.

5. **Publicize praise.** Just as a reprimand should always be given in private, praising should be done (whenever possible) in public. Sometimes the matter for which praise is given is a private issue, but it's more often appropriate to let your entire team in on the praise. If other team members are aware of the praise you give a colleague, it spurs them to work for similar recognition. In some cases, praise for significant accomplishments is extremely public, such as when it's given at meetings or company events.

Give Them Something to Keep

Telling people that you appreciate what they've done is a great idea, but *writing* it is even more effective. The aura of oral praise fades away; a letter or even a brief note endures. You don't have to spend much money. It doesn't take much time.

Write Thank-You Cards

At the A&G Merchandising Company in Wilmington, Delaware, team leaders are given packets of "thank you" cards on which the words *Thank You* are printed in beautiful script on the front flap, and the inside of the card is left blank. Whenever someone does something worthy of special recognition, that person's manager writes a note on one of the cards detailing the special accomplishment and congratulating the employee for achieving it. The recipients cherish the cards and show them to friends and family.

Plaques and Certificates

No matter what type of award you give to employees—large or small (cash, merchandise, tickets to a show or sports event, or a trip to a resort, for example)—it's worth spending a few more dollars to include a certificate or plaque. Employees love to hang these mementos in their cubicles or offices, over their workbenches, or in their homes. The cash gets spent, the merchandise wears out, the trip becomes a long-past memory, but a certificate or plaque is a permanent reminder of the recognition.

Chapter 9

Evaluating Performance

In This Chapter

➤ Setting performance standards

➤ Completing a formal performance appraisal

➤ Deciding whether to measure by traits or by results

➤ Conducting effective appraisal interviews

"How am I doing?" you ask your boss. Just as you want to know what your bosses think of your work, your team members are concerned about your opinion of their work. Most companies have periodic (usually annual) employee appraisals, but team leaders shouldn't wait for this formal review. Between appraisal sessions, you should talk to your team members regularly about their performance and make it an ongoing part of your coaching.

This chapter discusses how to set performance standards that are meaningful to team members and describes some of the techniques for measuring performance. You'll also learn how to conduct a formal appraisal interview.

Setting Standards

All employees should know just what's expected of them on the job. Many companies develop and incorporate *performance standards* at the time they create a job description. In other companies, a job evolves as standards are established.

In routine jobs, the key factors of performance standards involve quantity (how much should be produced per hour or per day) and quality (what level of quality is acceptable). As jobs become more complex, these standards aren't an adequate way to measure performance. Ideas and innovations that are conceived in creative jobs cannot be quantified, and quality may be difficult to measure. This situation doesn't mean that you can't have performance standards for these jobs, but it does require a different approach, such as the results-oriented evaluation system described later in this chapter.

Meanings and Gleanings

Performance standards define the results that are expected from a person performing a job. For performance standards to be meaningful, all persons doing that job should know and accept these standards.

Setting Criteria for Performance Standards

Performance standards are usually based on the experiences of satisfactory workers who have done that type of work over a length of time. Whether the standards cover quality or quantity of the work, or other aspects of the job, they should meet these criteria:

1. **Specific.** Every person doing a job should know exactly what he or she is expected to do.

2. **Measurable.** The company should have a touchstone against which performance can be measured. Measuring performance is easy when a standard is quantifiable; it's more difficult (but not impossible) when it isn't quantifiable. When a numerical measurement isn't feasible, some of the criteria may include timely completion of assignments, introduction of new concepts, or contribution to team activities.

3. **Realistic.** Unless standards are attainable, people consider them unfair and resist working toward them.

Self-Evaluation

When all team members know what's expected of them and against which standards they'll be measured, self-evaluation becomes almost automatic. Members don't have to wait for their team leader to tell them that they're below standard or behind schedule—they see that for themselves and can take corrective action immediately.

Self-evaluation makes a team leader's job easier. Like a good coach, he or she helps keep the team aware of the standards and provides support and encouragement to stay on target.

Formal Appraisals

Even if team members know the performance standards and can measure their own performance, and if team leaders reinforce this process with ongoing discussions about performance, there's still a need for formal appraisals. Most formal appraisals are conducted annually. Many team leaders add an informal appraisal semiannually or quarterly as a means of helping team members be aware of their progress.

This list describes some of the reasons that formal appraisals are important:

➤ They provide a framework for discussing a team member's overall work record. The team leader can use this meeting to recognize an employee for past successes and provide suggestions for even greater contributions.

➤ When they are objective, they enable team leaders to compare all members of the team against the same criteria.

➤ They provide helpful data for determining what type of additional training team members need.

➤ In many companies, they're the primary factor in determining salary increases and bonuses.

➤ Their formality causes them to be taken more seriously than informal comments about performance.

➤ They can be used as a vehicle for goal setting, career planning, and personal growth.

Secret Weapon

When rating team members, don't be overly influenced by their most recent behavior. At rating time, employees are as good as a kid just before Christmas. Keep a running log during the entire year.

The Downside of Performance Appraisals
Formal appraisals have some inherent problems, a few of which are as follow:

➤ They can be stressful for both leaders and team members.

➤ They make some team leaders so uncomfortable about making associates unhappy that the leaders overrate their performance.

➤ Many are inadequate, cumbersome, or poorly designed, which creates more problems than solutions.

➤ In some appraisals, good workers are underrated because their team leaders are afraid that team members might become competitors.

A properly managed performance appraisal can be a highly stimulating experience for both team members and team leaders. To make it most effective, don't treat it as a confrontation. Treat it instead as a meaningful two-way interchange that leads to an employee's commitment to reach out for improvement and to set goals for the coming year that will lead to a more productive and satisfying work experience.

Choosing the Best System

Your company may have in place an appraisal system that you are obligated to use. It may be helpful, however, to use aspects of other appraisal methods in addition to the method formally requested by your company. Many companies use an appraisal system that combines aspects of all the methods described here, so these aren't "pure" types.

Trait-Based Systems

The most common evaluation system is the "trait" format, in which a series of traits is listed in the left margin and each is measured against a scale from unsatisfactory to excellent.

Trait-based Appraisal Worksheet

	Excellent (5 points)	Very Good (4 points)	Average (3 points)	Needs Improvement (2 points)	Unsatisfactory (1 point)
Quantity of work					
Job knowledge					
Dependability					
Ability to take instruction					
Initiative					
Creativity					
Cooperation					

This system seems on the surface to be simple to administer and easy to understand, but it's loaded with problems:

➤ **A central tendency.** Rather than carefully evaluate each trait, it's much easier to rate a trait as average or close to average (the central rating).

➤ **The halo effect.** Some managers believe that one trait is so impressive that they rate all traits highly. Its opposite is the "pitchfork effect."

➤ **Personal biases.** Managers are human, and humans have personal biases for and against other people. These biases can influence any type of rating, but the trait system is particularly vulnerable.

➤ **Latest behavior.** It's easy to remember what employees have done during the past few months, but managers tend to forget what they did in the first part of a rating period.

Because the trait-based appraisal is measured in numerical terms, it is tempting to use the scores to compare employees. Some companies encourage the use of the bell curve in making these ratings. The bell-curve concept is based on the assumption that in a large population most people will fall in the average (middle) category, a smaller number in each of the poorer-than-average and better-than-average categories, and a still smaller number in the highest and lowest categories. The trouble with the use of the bell curve in employee evaluations is that small groups are unlikely to have this type of distribution—and it may work unfairly against top- and bottom-level workers.

Suppose that Carla is a genius who works in a department in which everyone is a genius. However, Carla is the lowest-level genius in the group. In a bell curve for that group, she would be rated as "poor." In any other group, she probably would be rated "superior."

Or, suppose that Harold's work is barely satisfactory but that his entire group is performing below average. Compared with the other employees, he's the best. If you use a bell curve, you have to rate him "superior."

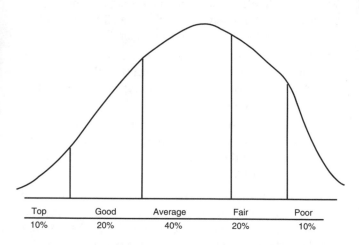

Bell Curve

Top	Good	Average	Fair	Poor
10%	20%	40%	20%	10%

Improving the System

The best way to overcome deficiencies in the trait system is to replace them with a results-oriented system (described later in this chapter). If your company does use the trait method, here are some suggestions to help make it more equitable:

➤ **Clarify standards.** Every manager and team leader should be carefully informed about the meaning of each category and the definition of each trait. Understanding quantity and quality is relatively easy. But what is dependability? How do you measure initiative, creativity, and other intangibles? By using discussions, role-plays, and case studies, you can develop standards that everyone understands and uses.

➤ **Establish criteria for ratings.** It's easy to identify superior and unsatisfactory employees, but it's tougher to differentiate among people in the middle three categories.

➤ **Keep a running log of member performance throughout the year.** You don't have to record average performance, but do note anything special that each member has accomplished or failed to accomplish. Some notes on the positive side may say, for example, "Exceeded quota by 20 percent," "Completed project two days before deadline," or "Made a suggestion that cut by a third the time required for a job." Notes on the negative side may say, "Had to redo report because of major errors" or "Was reprimanded for extending lunch hour three days this month."

➤ **Know yourself.** Make an effort to be aware of your personal biases and to overcome them.

➤ **Gather information.** Have specific examples of exceptional and unsatisfactory performance and behavior to back up your evaluation.

Measuring Results

Rather than rate team members on the basis of an opinion about their various traits, in this appraisal system the people who do the rating focus on the attainment of specific results. Results-based ratings can be used in any situation in which results are measurable. This system is obviously easier to use when quantifiable factors are involved (such as sales volume or production units), but it's also useful in such intangible areas as attaining specific goals in management development, reaching personal goals, and making collaborative efforts.

In a results-oriented evaluation system, the people who do the evaluating don't have to rely on their judgment of abstract traits, but instead can focus on what was expected from team members and how close they came to meeting these expectations. The expectations are agreed on at the beginning of a period and measured at the end of that period. At that time, new goals are developed to be measured at the end of the following period. Here's how this system works:

➤ For every job, the team leader and the people doing the job agree on the *KRAs (key results areas)* for that job. Employees must accomplish results in these areas to meet the team's goals.

➤ The team leader and the team member establish the results that are expected from the team member in each of the KRAs.

➤ During a formal review, the results an employee attained in each of the KRAs are measured against what was expected.

➤ A numerical scale is used in some organizations to rate employees on how closely they come to reaching their goals. In others, no grades are given. Instead, a narrative report is compiled to summarize what has been accomplished and to comment on its significance.

Meanings and Gleanings

A *KRA (key results area)* is an aspect of a job on which employees must concentrate time and attention to ensure that they achieve the goals for that job.

➤ Some companies request that team members submit monthly progress reports compiled in the same format as the annual review. This technique enables both the team member and the leader to monitor progress. By studying the monthly reports, the annual review is more easily compiled and discussed.

The Appraisal Interview

Regardless of whether you have evaluated employees by the trait method or the results method and whether they have made a self-evaluation, the most important facet of the appraisal process is the face-to-face discussion of the evaluation. To make this interview most valuable, you should carefully plan it and systematically carry it out.

Prepare Your Approach

Before sitting down with a team member to discuss a performance appraisal, study the evaluation. Make a list of all aspects you want to discuss —not just those that need improvement but also those in which the employee did good work. Study previous appraisals and note improvements that have been made since the preceding one. Prepare the questions you want to ask about past actions, steps to be taken for improvement, future goals, and how the team member plans to reach them.

Reflect on your experiences in dealing with this person. Have there been any special behavioral problems? Any problems that have affected her or his work? Any strong, positive assets you want to nurture? Any special points you want to discuss?

Discussing Performance

After you have made a team member feel at ease, point out the reasons for the appraisal meeting. Say something like this: "As you know, each year we review what has been accomplished during the preceding year and discuss what we can do together in the following year." Point out the areas of the job in which the team member has met standards, and particularly the areas in which he has excelled. By giving specific examples of these achievements, you let the team member know that you're aware of his positive qualities.

Because salary adjustment is usually based on overall performance, team members should be made aware that your praise of one or a few accomplishments isn't a guarantee of a raise. You might say, "The way you handled the *XYZ* account shows that you're making great progress. Keep up the good work." By saying it this way, you show that you're aware of the progress, but that there's still a ways to go. Rather than interpret the praise as "Wow, I'm good— this means a big raise," the reaction is, "I'm doing fine, but I'm not there yet."

Encourage team members to comment. Listen attentively, and then discuss the aspects of performance or behavior that didn't meet standards. Be specific. It's much more effective to give a few examples where expectations haven't been met than to just say, "Your work isn't up to snuff." Ask what team members plan to do to meet standards and what help they want you to provide.

Secret Weapon

When an employee rates himself higher than you do, don't get into a confrontation. Use specific examples to make your point.

If employees' problems aren't related to performance, but rather to behavior, provide examples: "During the past year, I've spoken to you several times about your tardiness. You're a good worker, and your opportunities in this company would be much greater if you could only get here on time all the time." Try to obtain a commitment and a plan of action to overcome this fault.

Constructive Criticism

Many managers find it difficult to give criticism. Here are some guidelines to help deal with this sensitive area:

➤ Begin with a positive approach by asking the team member to assess the successes achieved and the steps taken to achieve those successes.

➤ Encourage him or her to talk about projects that didn't succeed and what caused the failure.

➤ Ask what might have been done to avoid the mistakes made.

➤ Contribute your suggestions about how the matter could have been done more effectively.

➤ Ask what training or help you can provide.

➤ Agree on the steps the associate will take to ensure better performance on future assignments.

Secret Weapon

Allay people's fears about appraisal interviews by making some positive comments when you schedule an interview. Such as, "When we meet on Wednesday, I want to talk about your accomplishments this year and discuss our plans for next year."

Solicit Comments

Throughout interviews, encourage team members to comment on or make suggestions about every aspect of the review. Of course, they may have excuses or alibis. Listen empathetically—you may learn about some factors that have inhibited optimum performance. There may be factors within the company that keep an employee from performing adequately. For example, you may find out that someone has an older-model computer that has started "crashing" several times a day ever since the company upgraded software. You may not have been aware that this recurring problem was affecting the person's job performance. With this new information, you can take steps to correct the situation by budgeting for a computer upgrade.

By giving the person the opportunity to express his or her reasons or arguments, you can take steps to correct the situation. Even if a team member's excuses are superficial and self-serving, allowing them to be voiced clears the air. Then you both can be prepared to face real situations and come up with viable ideas.

Review Goals

If the preceding year's goals were met, congratulate the team member. Talk about the steps that were taken to meet goals and what was learned from this experience. If not all the goals were met, discuss any problems and the steps that might now be taken to overcome them.

An appraisal interview isn't just a review of the past—it's also a plan for the future. Ask the question, "What do you want to accomplish during the next twelve months?" The answer might include production goals, quality improvement, behavioral changes, and plans for advancement.

In addition to goals directly related to work, team members' future plans may include personal career-development plans (such as obtaining additional training on the job or in school), participation in trade or professional societies, and other off-job activities that can enhance a career. Be supportive of these types of goals, and point out what your company can do to help, such as providing tuition reimbursement. Don't make promises, however, or give false hopes for advancement or career growth that you can't deliver.

Have team members write down each of their goals and indicate next to them what they plan to do to achieve them. Give one copy to the team member and keep one with the performance-appraisal form. You can use it as part of the appraisal interview the following year.

Write an Action Plan

At the end of an interview, ask the team member to summarize the discussion. Make sure that the person fully understands the positive and negative aspects of his or her performance and behavior, plans and goals for the next review period, and any other pertinent matters. Keep a written record of these points.

In many companies, team members who disagree with an evaluation are given the opportunity to write a rebuttal to be attached to the appraisal. When salary adjustments are based on ratings, some organizations provide a procedure for appealing a review.

End the interview on a positive note by saying, "Overall, you've made good progress this year. I'm confident that you'll continue to do good work."

Record the Review

In most companies the appraisal form is sent to the human-resources department to be placed in the employee's personnel file. Some companies require that a copy be sent to the next level of management— the person to whom the team leader reports.

Even if it's not a formal practice in your company, it's a good idea to give a copy of the appraisal to the team member. It serves as a reminder of what was discussed at the appraisal interview and can be referred to during the year. And, as mentioned, if it includes goals the employee and you have agreed on for the year, the employee can re-read it from time to time to keep motivated.

When Reviewing Performance:

1. Know exactly what you want to achieve. Let your employees know what is expected of them.

2. Keep a record of employee performance from which to cite specific examples.

3. Discuss the written evaluation with the team member.

4. Listen to the team member's comments, then ask questions to stimulate thought.

5. Focus on the individual. Do not compare him or her with other members of the team.

6. Show that you care about employees' performance and their careers.

7. Reinforce good behavior. Be specific in your criticism. Give examples from their performance record. Ask them how they can do even better. Add your own suggestions.

8. Focus on the behavior, not on the person.

9. Don't be afraid to give honest criticism. Most employees want to know where they stand and how to improve.

10. Help team members set personal goals that are congruent with the goals of the team and the company and develop a plan of action to reach those goals.

Secret Weapon

In the evaluation interview, concentrate on the work, not on the person. Never say, "You were no good." Say instead, "Your work didn't meet standards."

Chapter 10

Counseling Employees

In This Chapter

➤ Helping people who don't like themselves

➤ Dealing with problem employees

➤ Confronting alcohol- and drug-abuse problems

➤ Gripes and grievances

➤ Employee assistance programs

Your team is made up of people—human beings—who bring to their jobs skills, intelligence, and creativity. But people also have idiosyncrasies, attitudes, moods, and problems—and they also bring those things to the job. One of the great challenges of being a leader lies in recognizing and dealing with these types of problems so that your department will run smoothly.

Building Up Self-Esteem

Consider the phrase "developing self-esteem." Many people who have had a low opinion of themselves have been able to overcome it by making a commitment to make a change. Sometimes they seek professional help, but often they do it through self-determination: They re-write the script on which they base their life. As a team leader, you're in a position to help such people develop self-esteem.

People with low *self-esteem* are more likely to complain about their failures than to brag about successes. They rarely express opinions that differ from those of other team members. When pressed to express their thoughts or ideas, they start their answers with, "I'm not sure about this" or "I'm probably wrong, but...." They never volunteer to lead a discussion, and they take charge of a project only when the leader assigns it and then they express doubts about their ability to do it properly.

Meanings and Gleanings

Self-esteem refers to the way you feel about yourself. If you think of yourself as a success, you will be a success; if you think of yourself as second rate, you will always be second rate—unless you change your self-perception.

A person's low self-esteem (or worse, self-loathing) unfortunately may have deep psychological roots that stem from childhood. Parents may instill this trait in their children by being overdemanding (for example, if Jason gets a test score of 90 percent and his parents berate him for not getting 100 percent, or if Sarah is a talented pianist but her parents deride her playing because she's not a child prodigy). Jason and Sarah are likely to write scripts for themselves as failures, doomed always to be inadequate. People whose scripts are based on parental belittlement need professional assistance to overcome it.

Keep a Success Log

One technique involves keeping a success log. Enter in this log any accomplishments you're especially proud of—things for which you've been commended. These things prove that you've succeeded in the past and serve as your assurance that you can succeed again.

Secret Weapon

Keep a success log for your team. Enter in it the special achievements of each of your team members and of your team as a whole. When things don't go well, have everyone reread the log.

More Tools for Building Up Self-Esteem

In addition to maintaining success logs, you can help team members build their self-esteem in other ways:

➤ Give them positive reinforcement for every achievement, and praise for progress made in their work. Be positive when they come up with a good idea or make meaningful contributions to team discussions and activities. People with low self-esteem need to be continually reminded that you, the team leader, respect them and have confidence in them.

➤ Give them assignments that you know they can handle, and provide added training, coaching, and support to ensure that they'll succeed. The taste of success is a sure-fire way to build self-esteem.

➤ Suggest that they take courses designed to build self-confidence, such as the Dale Carnegie Course or assertiveness-training programs. Provide them with inspirational tapes or books.

If, despite these efforts, a person doesn't become more self-confident, professional help may be necessary. Suggest that he or she see a counselor in your employee assistance program

Alcohol and Drugs

Suppose that one of your team members seems to have an alcohol problem. You've never seen the person drink or come to work drunk, but you often smell alcohol on the person's breath. He or she is frequently absent, especially on Mondays. You can't ignore this situation. Speak to the team member about it, and prepare to hear all sorts of denials: "Me, drink? Only socially." Or, "Alcohol breath? It's cough medicine."

Rather than talk about a drinking problem, talk about job performance, absence from work, and other job-related matters. Inform the person that if the situation continues, you'll have to take disciplinary action. If your team member continues this behavior pattern, bring up your concern about the drinking and suggest—or insist on—counseling.

Discussing Alcohol Problems

It isn't easy to discuss with a team member such a sensitive and personal matter as an alcohol problem. The U.S. Department of Health and Human Services suggests the following approach, in its pamphlet *Supervisor's Guide on Alcohol Abuse*.

➤ **Don't apologize for discussing the matter.** Make it clear that job performance is involved.

➤ **Encourage your team member to explain why work performance, behavior, or attendance is deteriorating.** This approach may provide an opportunity to discuss the use of alcohol.

➤ **Don't discuss a person's right to drink or make a moral issue of it.** Alcoholism is a disease that, left untreated, can lead to many more serious illnesses.

➤ **Don't suggest that your team member use moderation or change drinking habits.** According to Alcoholics Anonymous, alcoholics cannot change their drinking habits without help. It's up to them to make the decision to stop drinking and take steps to get that help.

➤ **Don't be distracted by excuses for drinking.** The problem as far as you're concerned is the drinking itself—and how it affects work, behavior, attendance, and performance on the job.

➤ **Remember that alcoholics, like any other sick people, should be given the opportunity for treatment and rehabilitation.**

➤ **Emphasize that your primary concern is the team member's work performance.** Point out that if the person's behavior doesn't improve, you'll have to take disciplinary action, including suspension or discharge.

➤ **Point out that the decision to seek assistance is the team member's responsibility.** If your company has an employee assistance program, describe it and strongly recommend that it be used.

Secret Weapon

To prevent any misunderstandings or ambiguities, every company should have a written policy prohibiting drinking on company premises or during working hours.

Preventive Steps

In most companies, showing up at work drunk or drinking on the job is a punishable offense. But it's not always easy to prove that a person is drunk. Appearing to be drunk isn't enough. Even a police officer cannot arrest a suspect for driving while intoxicated, unless he or she substantiates the claim with a breath or blood test.

If one of your employees seems to be drunk, your safest course is to send the person to your medical department for testing. If that's not possible, don't allow the person to work—send him or her home. The next day, discuss the situation and point out that if it reoccurs, you'll take disciplinary action. Also, make sure to suggest counseling.

Secret Weapon

If you send drunk people home, don't let them drive. If they get into an accident, you or your company may share liability. Call a taxi.

Although drug use on the job has increased, it isn't nearly as common as drinking. Treat drug users the same way you deal with drinkers. Because drug use (and particularly the sale of drugs) is illegal, however, you should consult your attorney about the best ways to handle this situation. Testing for the use of drugs is becoming an increasingly routine practice in many companies. A survey of more than 3,500 companies showed that 48 percent test job applicants and that 43 percent periodically test employees. Although some companies do conduct random drug tests, most of them test employees only when they suspect drug use. The ADA (Americans with Disabilities

Act) includes alcoholism and drug addiction as disabilities (see Chapter 6, "Equal Employment Laws").

Counseling

It takes the coordinated effort of all team members to keep your team operating at optimum capacity. It takes only one member of the team who isn't functioning effectively to prevent your team from achieving its objectives. As coach of the team, you must identify problems in their early stages and correct the situation before it mushrooms into a major problem. Your tool: *counseling.*

Meanings and Gleanings

Counseling is a means of helping troubled associates overcome barriers to good performance. By careful listening, open discussion, and sound advice, a counselor helps identify problems, clarify misunderstandings, and plan solutions.

When a team leader counsels an associate, it's more analogous to a coach of an athletic team counseling a player than to a psychotherapist counseling a patient. Professional counseling should be done by trained specialists, and, as you will learn in this chapter, sometimes referrals to these specialists are necessary.

Gripes and Grievances

Sometimes you see a problem; sometimes you don't. You find out only when someone complains. A complaint may be your first hint of an impending problem, a reminder of an ongoing situation that hasn't been attended to; or it may just be one of your associates letting off steam. But you don't know until you check it out.

Chronic Complainers

You know your team members. Some of them are always complaining. They gripe about the temperature in the room and the work they're assigned. Such people get their kicks from complaining. Sometimes they do have legitimate complaints, so you can't just automatically ignore them. You have to listen—and that can be time-consuming and annoying.

One way to minimize this kind of griping is to pay more attention to the people who complain. The reason for the complaints is often their desire to be the center of attention. By talking to them, asking their opinions, and praising their good work, you satisfy their need for attention and give them less reason to gripe.

Check Out Complaints

Even if a complaint seems to have no validity, check it out anyway. You may discover facets of the situation you weren't aware of. Take care of *gripes* before they become *grievances*.

1. **Listen.** Even if a complaint seems to be unfounded, in the mind of the complainant it's a serious matter.

2. **Investigate.** Take nothing for granted. Look at the record and talk to others who know about the situation.

3. **Report back.** If the gripe is unfounded, explain your reasoning to the complainant. If it *is* substantiated, explain what you will do to correct it.

4. **Take action.** Do what must be done to correct the problem.

Meanings and Gleanings

A *gripe* is an informal complaint. A *grievance* is a formal complaint, usually based on the violation of a union contract or formal company policy.

Correcting the Problem

Suppose that a complainer is correct: Your investigation verifies that the complaint is justified. Fix it if you can, but often it's not within your power to do it. Find out who can. Bring the situation to the attention of your boss or whoever can adjust it.

Diana was frustrated. When she described to her boss, Charles, a problem her team members were having, he promised to rectify it but never did. Diana's reminders were rebuffed. She was concerned about not only having to continue to work with this unsatisfactory situation but also losing the respect of her team members. She discussed the situation with Elizabeth, a manager who had been her mentor earlier in her career.

Elizabeth's advice: "Let Charles know how important it is to your team to have someone listen to their complaints and consider them seriously. Remind Charles that you deal with every problem over which you have authority, but that this one is out of your jurisdiction. Point out that you screen all complaints and don't pass on the ones that aren't justified. If there's a reason that action has not or cannot be taken, you want to know so that you can pass on the information to your team. Tell him that they're reasonable people who understand that they can't get everything they want, but that they expect that their complaints will be taken seriously. Then let your associates know what action you're taking and what results from it."

Secret Weapon

As tempting as it may be to threaten to fire uncooperative team members, don't do it unless you really can carry it out. Union contracts or legal implications may restrict these actions.

Formal Grievances

When a company has a union contract, the procedures for handling grievances are clearly outlined. Companies that don't have union agreements often set up their own procedures for dealing with employee grievances. Here's a typical four-step approach:

1. The person making the complaint discusses it with his or her immediate supervisor or team leader. Every attempt to resolve the problem should be made at this level.

2. If no settlement is reached, the individual should be given an opportunity to bring the problem to the next level of management without fear of reprisal.

3. If the complaint is still unresolved, it may go to the general manager or a specially appointed manager (often the human-resources director). An agreement is usually reached during this stage.

4. Although arbitration is rare in a nonunion environment, the management in some companies provides for a mutually agreed-upon third party to be

available if the company and the aggrieved person cannot work out their problem.

As the immediate supervisor or team leader, you play the key role in this process. You should make every effort to resolve grievances without having to go beyond step 1. Grievance procedures take time and energy that would be better used doing your team's primary work.

Secret Weapon

No complaints doesn't mean that there are no problems. It may indicate that communications are blocked. If no one attends to grievances and gripes, they fester in the minds of the aggrieved and burst out later. Keep those channels open.

Preventing Grievances

Dealing with grievances is time-consuming and takes you away from more productive work. This section provides some suggestions for preventing grievances from developing on your team:

➤ Regularly let all team members know how they're doing. People want feedback on not only their failures but also their successes.

➤ Encourage team members to participate in all aspects of planning and performing the team's work.

➤ Listen to team members' ideas.

➤ Make only promises that you know you can keep.

➤ Be alert to minor irritations and trivial problems so that you can correct them before they fester into serious dissatisfactions.

➤ Resolve problems as soon as possible after hearing about them.

Resolving Conflicts

Suppose that you give an assignment to two of your team members, Ken and Barbie. They discuss the project and cannot agree about how it should be pursued. They both come back to you, their team leader, to resolve the problem. You can use one of two approaches: arbitration or mediation.

Mediation

Mediation is the preferred approach because it's more likely to result in a win-win compromise. The most negative effect of using mediation is that it's time-consuming (and you often don't have much time to solve a problem).

Suppose that you have chosen to mediate the disagreement between Ken and Barbie. To make a mediated conflict resolution work, all parties involved must be fully aware of the procedure to be followed. *Unless both parties have a clear understanding of the approach, it cannot succeed.*

1. First, Barbie tells how she views the situation. (You might think that the next step is for Ken to state his side—but it isn't.)

2. Ken states Barbie's view as he understands it.
   The reason for this step is that when the Barbie explains her view to Ken, typically he will only partly listen. He may be thinking about what to say next and how to rebut the argument.

   By being aware of having to repeat the first person's views, the listener becomes aware of having to listen carefully.

   When Ken repeats Barbie's side of the story, any areas of misunderstanding can be clarified before he presents his views. It's amazing how often conflicts are caused by these types of misunderstandings.

3. The same process is then followed with Ken stating his views.

4. During this discussion, you (as the mediator) take notes. After Barbie and Ken present their views, you review your notes with the participants. You might say, "As I see this, you both agree on 80 percent of the project. Now let's list the areas in which you disagree." Most disputes have many more areas of agreement than disagreement. By identifying these areas, you can focus on matters that must be resolved and tackle them one at a time.

Because you don't have an unlimited amount of time, you must set a time limit on these meetings. Suppose that you've set aside two hours for the first meeting. At the end of the specified time, you still have several more items to discuss. Set up another meeting for that purpose. Suggest that the participants meet in the interim without you to work on some of the problems. Often, after a climate of compromise is established, a large number of issues can be resolved without your presence.

Secret Weapon

Don't give advice about serious personal matters. Listen! Help put the problem into perspective. Suggest sources for additional information. Help clarify a situation.

Now the next meeting is scheduled for one hour, and more problems are resolved. If the project must get under way, this may be all the time you have. If some unresolved problems still exist, you have to change your role from mediator to arbitrator and make the decisions.

Arbitration

The following five steps can help you *arbitrate* a conflict, if you choose to deal with it in that way:

1. **Get the facts.** Listen carefully to both sides. Investigate on your own to get additional information. Don't limit yourself to "hard facts." Learn about underlying feelings and emotions.

2. **Evaluate the facts.**

3. **Study the alternatives.** Are the solutions suggested by the two parties the only possible choices? Can compromises be made? Is a different resolution possible?

4. **Make a decision.**

5. **Notify the two parties of your decision.** Make sure that they fully understand it. If necessary, "sell" it to them so that they will agree and be committed to implementing it.

Meanings and Gleanings

In *arbitration*, both parties present their cases and an arbitrator decides what should be done. In *mediation*, both parties present their cases and a mediator works with them to reach a mutually satisfactory solution.

When Talking Doesn't Help

When job problems are caused by alcoholism or drug addiction, there's little you can do other than encourage or even insist on appropriate programs. When the real cause stems from deep-seated emotional factors, professional help is necessary.

You may be reluctant or even embarrassed to suggest that a team member see a professional counselor. Many people take umbrage at this suggestion: "Do you think I'm nuts?" Point out that going to a professional counselor is now as accepted as going to a medical doctor. Young people are exposed to counseling beginning in elementary school. The most frequently given advice offered by Ann Landers, Dear Abby, and other advice columnists is to seek counseling when faced with serious problems.

Not all problems that require professional assistance are psychological. They may be caused by a medical condition or serious financial troubles. Often they're marital or family situations.

If your company has an EAP (employee assistance program), making a referral to it immediately relieves you of the burden of suggesting specific counseling (see the following section). If not, your human-resources department may help provide referrals. You may find it helpful to research the available sources of help in your community:

➤ **Medical doctors.** If a company doesn't have its own medical department or an employee doesn't have a primary-care physician, local hospitals or medical societies can provide a list of qualified physicians.

➤ **Psychiatrists.** These M.D.s deal with serious psychological disorders.

➤ **Psychologists or psychotherapists.** These specialists usually have a degree in psychology or social work and handle most of the usual emotional problems people face.

➤ **Marriage counselors and family therapists.** These professionals deal with marital problems, difficulties with children, and related matters. Obtain from your local family-service association or mental-health association the names of qualified psychologists, psychiatrists, or marriage and family therapists in your area.

➤ **Financial counselors.** These people help others work out payment plans with creditors, develop budgets, and live within their income. Your bank or credit union can provide referrals.

Secret Weapon

When you refer someone for professional help, avoid using the terms "psychiatrist," "psychologist," or "therapist." Suggest that he or she might benefit from seeing a counselor who specializes in a particular area.

Employee Assistance Programs (EAPs)

An employee assistance program, or EAP, is a company-sponsored counseling service. Many companies have instituted these programs to help employees deal with personal problems that interfere with productivity. The counselors aren't company employees, but instead are outside experts retained on an as-needed basis. Initiating the use of the EAP can be done in two ways:

1. The employee takes the initiative in contacting the company's EAP. The company informs its employees about the program through bulletins, announcements in the company newspaper, meetings, e-mail, and letters to their homes. Often a hot-line telephone number is provided.

Gerty believes that she needs help. Constant squabbling with her teenage daughter has made her tense, angry, and frustrated. In a brief telephone interview with her company's EAP, the screening counselor identifies Gerty's problem and refers her to a family counselor. Gerty makes her own appointment on her own time (not during working hours—EAPs are not an excuse for taking time off the job). Because the entire procedure is confidential, no report is made to the company about the counseling (in most cases, not even the names of people who undertake counseling are divulged).

2. Another way to start the process is by having a supervisor take the initiative to contact the EAP. Suppose that the work performance of one of your top performers has recently declined. You often see him sitting idly at his desk, his thoughts obviously far from his job. You ask him what's going on, but he shrugs off your question by saying, "I'm okay—just tired."

   After several conversations, he finally tells you about a family problem, and you suggest that he contact your company's EAP.

Even though you've made the referral and the employee has followed through, don't expect progress reports. From now on, the matter is handled confidentially. Your feedback comes from seeing improvement in the employee's work as the counseling helps with the problem.

Employee assistance programs are expensive to maintain, but organizations that have used them for several years report that they pay off. EAPs salvage skilled and experienced workers who, without help, may leave a company.

Chapter 11

Discipline

In This Chapter

➤ The steps of progressive discipline

➤ How and when to reprimand

➤ Written warnings

➤ Probation and suspension

When you hear or see the word *discipline*, the first thing that usually pops into your mind is punishment. Look at that word again. Notice that by dropping just two letters (*i* and *n*), it turns into *disciple*, a synonym for "student." Both words are derived from the Latin word meaning "to learn." If you look at discipline not as punishment but as a means of learning, both you and your associates get much more out of it. You are the *coach*, and your associates are the *learners*.

Unfortunately, people don't always learn what they are taught. Sometimes, despite your best efforts, some people on your team may not perform satisfactorily. If infractions still occur, even after you've clearly explained the rules, you must take steps to get things back on track. Regardless of the cause, discipline begins when you work to correct the problem. When you've made every effort to help your associates learn and when all else fails, only then does discipline take the form of punishment.

Keep in mind that the contents of this chapter are based on general practices that are used in many organizations. Your company's policies may differ. You may get some good ideas from this chapter that you can't use now, but you can suggest them to your company's management. Until your company incorporates these ideas into its policies, however, follow your company's current practices.

Progressive Discipline

In most organizations, it's important for every member of a team to be at his or her workstation at starting time. If one person comes to work late, it can hold up an entire team.

Meanings and Gleanings

Progressive discipline is a systematic approach to correcting rule infractions. A typical program has six steps: an informal warning followed by a disciplinary interview, written warning, probation, suspension, and termination (if necessary).

Suppose that an employee was late three times in his first month on the job. You spoke to him about it, and for several months he kept his promise to be on time. Now he begins to regress. He was late one day last week, and this morning he was late again. His reason for the tardiness is vague. Your informal chats with him about the matter haven't done any good. The next step is to apply *progressive discipline.*

The Reprimand

Those chats you've had with the team member about his lateness weren't part of the progressive discipline system; instead, they were a friendly reminder of his responsibility to your team.

The first official step in the progressive discipline system is often called the "oral," or "verbal," warning: You take the team member aside and remind him that the two of you have discussed his lateness and that, because he continues to come to work late, you must put him on notice. Inform him of the next steps you'll take if the behavior continues

You may be exasperated about a team member's failure to keep a promise to be on time. It's normal to be annoyed if your team's work is delayed, but don't lose your cool. A typical conversation shows you what *not* to do:

> You (angrily): How many times do I have to tell you that we need you here at 8 o'clock? You know that we have a deadline to meet today. Haven't you any sense of responsibility?
>
> Employee (annoyed): I was only ten minutes late. It's not my fault—I ran into a traffic problem.
>
> You: If you had left home early enough, you wouldn't have had a traffic problem. The rest of us were here on time. You just don't have a sense of responsibility.
>
> Employee: I have as much of a sense of responsibility as anyone.
>
> You: If you're late again, I'll write you up.

Did this conversation solve anything? The objective of an informal warning is to alert team members that a problem needs correction. By using an angry tone and antagonistic attitude, you only rile the person and avoid solving the problem.

Let's replay that reprimand in a better way:

> You: You know how important it is for you to be here when the workday begins. The entire team depends on all of us being on time.
>
> Employee: I'm sorry. I ran into unusual traffic this morning.
>
> You: We all face traffic in the morning. What can you do to make sure that you'll be on time in the future?
>
> Employee: I've tried alternative routes, but it doesn't help. I guess I'll have to leave earlier every day so that, if I do run into traffic, I'll at least have a head start.
>
> You: That sounds good to me. You're a valuable member of our team, and being on time will help all of us.

When you're preparing to reprimand someone, to ensure that you conduct the reprimand in the most effective manner, review the guidelines for reprimanding below.

Secret Weapon

Never reprimand people when you're angry, when they're angry, or in the presence of other people. Reprimands should be a private matter between two calm people working together to solve a problem.

Guidelines for Reprimanding

Time the reprimand properly. As soon as possible after the offense has been committed, call the employee aside and discuss the matter in private.

Never reprimand when you're angry. Wait until you have calmed down.

Emphasize the *what*, not the *who*. Base the reprimand on the action that was wrong, not on the person.

Begin by stating the problem and then ask a question. Don't begin with an accusation: "You're always late!" Say instead, "You know how important it is for all of us to be on the job promptly. What can you do to get here on time from now on?"

Listen! Attentive, open-minded listening is one of the most important factors of true leadership. Ask questions to elicit as much information about the situation as you can. Respond to the associate's comments, but don't convert the interview into a confrontation.

Encourage your team member to make suggestions for solving the problem. When a person participates in reaching a solution, there's a much greater chance that it will be accepted and accomplished.

Provide constructive criticism. Give your team member specific suggestions, when possible, about how to correct a situation.

Never use sarcasm. Sarcasm never corrects a situation; it only makes the other person feel inadequate and put-upon.

End your reprimand on a positive note. Comment on some of the good things the person has accomplished so that he or she knows that you're not focusing only on the reason for this reprimand, but instead on total performance. Reassure the person that you look on him or her as a valuable member of your team.

Excuses

If you've been in management for any length of time, you've probably heard some wild excuses. No matter how improbable the excuse may be, listen carefully—for these reasons:

> ➤ Until you listen to the entire story, you cannot know whether it has validity. In most companies, there are acceptable reasons for not following a company rule or procedure. Under extenuating circumstances, it's sensible to be flexible when you enforce the rules.

> ➤ Even if an excuse is unacceptable, let your team member get it out of his or her system (a process called *catharsis*). When people have something on their mind, they won't listen to a word you say until they get their story out. Whether it's a team member's tardiness or a customer's complaint, let the person talk. Only after a person's mind is clear will he or she listen to you. Afterward, you can say, "I understand what you're saying, but the important thing is to be here on time."

Plan of Action

When you deliver a verbal warning, throw the problem back to your team member. Rather than say, "This is what you should do," ask "What do you think you can do to correct this situation?" Get people to come up with their own plans of action.

In a simple situation such as tardiness, a plan of action is easy to develop: "I'll leave my house fifteen minutes earlier every day." In more complex situations, a plan may take longer to develop. You may suggest that the person think about the problem for a day or so and arrange a second meeting in which to present and discuss a plan.

Documenting a Reprimand

Even an informal reprimand shouldn't be strictly oral. You should keep a record of it. Legal implications mandate that you document any action that could lead to serious disciplinary action. Some team leaders document an informal warning by simply noting it on their calendars or entering it in a team log. Others write a detailed memo for their files. You should use the technique your company prefers.

The Disciplinary Interview

If an employee repeats an offense after receiving a verbal warning, the next step is the disciplinary interview. This interview is more formal than a reprimand. A verbal warning is usually a relatively brief session, often conducted in a quiet corner of the room. A disciplinary interview is longer and is conducted in an office or conference room.

A disciplinary interview should always be carefully prepared and result in a mutually agreed-upon plan of action. Whereas a plan of action after a verbal warning is usually oral, the resulting plan in a disciplinary interview should be put in writing. It not only reminds both the leader and the team member of what has been agreed on, but also serves as documentation. To ensure that a disciplinary interview is carried out systematically, use the discipline worksheet in Appendix B.

Secret Weapon

Be alert for any deviations from standards before they become problems. By dealing with rule infractions early on, you can usually avoid disciplinary procedures.

Writing Up Warnings

The next step in progressive discipline is to give the offender a written warning—a letter or form that will be placed in his or her personnel file. Written warnings often are taken more seriously than the first two steps. Employees don't want negative reports in their personnel files, and even the possibility that they'll be "written up" serves as a deterrent to poor behavior.

If the written warning concerns poor performance, specify the performance standards and indicate in what way the employee's performance fell short of the standards. Also state what was done to help the employee meet the standards. This will protect you against potential claims that you made no effort to bring the performance up to standard. If the warning concerns infraction against a company rule, specify the nature of the offense and what disciplinary steps were taken before the warning was written (see the following two sample letters).

Memo for Poor Conduct

From (team leader): _____ Date: _____

To: _____

On (date) _____ , we had a discussion concerning _____
_____
_____

At that time, you agreed to _____

Because you have not complied with this agreement, you are being formally notified that if the above matter is not corrected by (date)_____ , additional disciplinary steps will be taken as specified in Section ____ of the Policies and Procedures manual.

Signed (team leader): _____

Team member's comments: _____
_____
_____

Signed (team member): _____

To protect your company from potential legal problems, check any form letters concerning discipline with your legal advisors before sending them to be printed. Although it's always advantageous from a legal standpoint to have employees sign *all* disciplinary documents, it becomes imperative when the warning itself is in writing.

You can't force anyone to sign anything. If an employee refuses to sign a disciplinary document, call in a witness— a person who is not directly involved in the situation— and repeat your request. If he or she still refuses, have the witness attest to that response on the document.

To avoid misunderstandings, give copies of all disciplinary documents to the employee. You should send a copy to the human resources department to include in the person's personnel file. Whether the reason for discipline is poor conduct or poor performance, refer to the sample letters in this chapter for ideas about how to phrase a written warning.

Memo for Poor Performance

From (team leader): _____ Date: _____

To (team member): _____

The performance standard for (specify job) _____ is (specify standard in quantity, quality, or other terms) _____

_____

_____

Your performance has not met these standards (give details): _____

_____

To help you, I gave you ____ hours of special coaching. The areas covered include:

_____

_____

Signed (team leader): _____

Team member's comments: _____

Signed (team member): _____

Probation

Until now all your attempts to correct a team member's performance or behavior have been positive, and you've provided advice and counsel. If nothing has worked, your next step is to put the team member on probation. Set a deadline for adjusting the situation. What you're doing is giving your associate one more chance to shape up before you invoke some form of punishment. Most people take probation seriously—they know that you mean business.

The two primary reasons for progressive discipline are (1) poor performance and (2) poor conduct. If performance is a problem, probation is the last step before termination. If all the retraining, counseling, and coaching you give a team member fails, you can give the person one last chance to overcome the problem over a probationary period. If that doesn't help, additional disciplinary steps won't help. If you can transfer the person to a more suitable job, do so; if not, you have no other choice than to terminate him or her.

Company practices for administering *probation* vary considerably. They're governed by union contracts, company-policy manuals, or sometimes unwritten (but previously followed) practices. Usually the notification of probation is in the form of a written statement, signed by the team leader or a higher-ranking manager and acknowledged by the employee. The employee keeps one copy; the team leader gets another copy; and the human-resources department keeps a copy in its files.

Meanings and Gleanings

Putting a team member on *probation* for a specified period of time gives him or her another chance to improve performance or correct unsatisfactory behavior. If the improvement is not made, the next step in the progressive discipline system is taken.

Probationary periods vary from as few as ten days to the more customary thirty days and sometimes even longer. If an employee makes significant progress, lift the probation. If he or she repeats the offense after the probation is lifted, you can either reinstate the probation or invoke the next step.

When an offense violates company rules (tardiness, absenteeism, or other misconduct), proceed to the next step, which is usually suspension.

Suspension

You're severely limited in the ways you can punish employees. Ever since flogging was abolished, only a few types of punishment can be legally administered. The most commonly used method, short of termination, is suspension without pay. Although team leaders often have some leeway in determining the length of a suspension, most companies set specific suspension times depending on the seriousness of the offense.

The mechanics of issuing a suspension are similar to that of probation. Because suspension is a much more serious step, union contracts often mandate consultation with a union representative before suspending an employee. Companies that aren't unionized require approval for suspensions by both the manager to whom the team leader reports and the human-resources department.

Appropriate documentation specifying the reason for the suspension and the exact period of time involved should be made, signed by the appropriate manager, and acknowledged by the suspended employee. If an employee returns from a suspension and continues to break the rules, your next step may be a longer suspension or even termination.

Secret Weapon

The downside of suspending a team member is that you lose that person's contribution to the team effort during the suspension period. Make every effort to keep the person employed by training and counseling so that suspension isn't necessary.

Termination

The chief purpose of progressive discipline is to give the offending employee an opportunity to change his or her behavior and become a productive, cooperative team member. Take stricter steps only after less strict steps have failed to solve the problem. The objective is to help the person succeed so that termination isn't necessary. If the employee fails to improve, however, the termination should take place.

Chapter 12

Separation and Termination

In This Chapter

➤ Terminating someone after progressive discipline

➤ Terminating employees spontaneously

➤ Employment at will

➤ Voluntary resignations

Terminating employees is a serious matter that always needs careful consideration. In most companies, before a supervisor or team leader can terminate anyone, approval must be obtained from both the person to whom the leader reports and the human-resources department. This step is important to ensure that company policies and legal requirements are fully observed. This chapter examines the importance of this process.

Caution!

What you say and how you say it are important. Because the issue of firing employees is such a sensitive one, you must do it diplomatically and be fully aware of any legal implications. Ask your human resources department for advice about dealing with this situation.

Some team leaders get more upset about having to fire someone than the person who is being fired. Here are some suggestions to help you prepare:

➤ Review all documents so that you're fully aware of all the reasons and implications involved in the decision to terminate the team member.

➤ Review all that you know about the team member's personality:

- What problems have you had with the person?
- How did he or she respond to the preceding disciplinary steps?
- How did you and the team member get along on the job?
- How did he or she relate to other team members?
- What personal problems does the person have that you're aware of?

➤ Review any problems you've had in firing other employees and map out a plan to avoid those problems.

➤ Check your company's policy manual or discuss with the human-resources department any company rules that apply.

➤ Relax before the meeting. Do whatever helps you clear your mind and calm your emotions. If you've done your job correctly, you've made every effort to help the team member succeed. The progressive discipline system has given the person several chances to change, so you don't have to feel guilty about the firing.

Secret Weapon

If an employee raises his or her voice, lower yours. Most people respond to a raised voice by raising their own. By responding in a soft voice, you disarm the other person.

It's Showtime!

You've stalled as long as you can. Now you're ready to sit down with the employee and make it clear that this is the end of the line. Find a private place to conduct the meeting. Your office is an obvious spot, but it may not be the best one. A conference room is better because, if the fired employee breaks down or becomes belligerent, you can walk out.

Most people who are fired expect it and don't cause problems. They may beg for another chance, but this isn't the time to change your mind. Don't let the termination meeting degenerate into a confrontation. If the employee gives you a hard time, keep cool. Don't lose your temper or get into an argument.

It's a good idea to have another person in the room at a termination meeting. A person being fired may say or do inappropriate things. Also, you may become upset and say something that's best left unsaid. The presence of a third person keeps both you and the employee from losing your temper and from saying or doing something that can lead to additional complications.

The best "third person" in a termination meeting is a representative from the human-resources department. If such a person isn't available, call in another manager or team leader. If the employee belongs to a union, the union contract usually stipulates the presence of a union delegate.

Having a third person in the room when you terminate an employee also provides a witness if an employee later sues your company. Suppose that a former employee files an age-discrimination suit several weeks after being fired for poor performance. She claims that during the termination meeting, you stated that the company needs younger people in order to meet production standards. Although the claim is false, you'll have to spend time, energy, and money to defend against it—and it's your word against the other person's. If a third person is present at termination meetings, former employees will be less likely to file false claims because they know that they'll be refuted by a witness.

Secret Weapon

Because terminations may be challenged in court, keep complete records and appropriate documentation for all steps that led to the termination.

In most organizations, when a termination meeting ends, the employee is sent to the human-resources department for outprocessing, or handling the administrative details for completing the separation procedure. In some situations, the supervisor must handle this at the time of termination. Be sure to follow the company's procedures carefully. As a guide, use the termination checklist in Appendix B to ensure that you take the necessary steps in terminating an employee.

Spontaneous Termination

Occasionally, termination without warning is permitted. These occasions are rare and usually limited to a few serious infractions that are clearly delineated in company policies. Serious offenses include drinking on the job, fighting, stealing, and insubordination. Because these charges aren't always easy to prove, be very careful before you make the decision to fire someone without progressive discipline. You must have solid evidence that can stand up in court. Law books are loaded with cases in which people who, after being fired, have sued former employers for unlawful discharge, defamation of character, false imprisonment, and whatever else their lawyers could dream up.

Insubordination, which is one of the most frequent causes of spontaneous termination, isn't always easy to prove. If an employee simply fails to carry out an order, it's not grounds enough for termination. Unless a failure to obey instructions can lead to serious consequences, it's better to use progressive discipline. On the other hand, if a team member becomes unruly in his or her refusal (if he or she hollers and screams or spits in your face, for example), spontaneous discharge may be appropriate.

Secret Weapon

As angry as you may be about the trouble an employee has caused or how nasty he or she may be, don't use the termination meeting to tell the person off.

Documenting Spontaneous Discharge

When you fire someone after progressive-discipline procedures fail, you have an entire series of documents to back you up. In spontaneous termination, however, you have no documents. Immediately after a termination, write a detailed report describing the circumstances that led up to it. Get written statements from witnesses. If you can, get the employee to sign a statement presenting his or her side of the story. In the event that this discharge is challenged, having the terminated employee's immediate comments will protect you in case he or she presents a different version of what happened.

Meanings and Gleanings

When an employee quits because of intentional unfair treatment on the job, it is "constructed" by the courts to be equivalent to being fired and is referred to as *constructive discharge.*

Employment at Will

Unless you have a personal contract with your employer or are covered by a contract with a union, you and all your team members are "employees at will." This concept has governed employment since colonial times. Bosses always had the right to fire employees, and, ever since slavery was abolished, employees could always quit. Only recently has this concept been challenged.

To understand *employment at will,* you first have to know a little about our legal system. Americans are subject to two kinds of law: legislated acts and common law. The former are the laws passed by Congress, the states, and local governments. Common law is based on accepted practices as interpreted by court decisions over the years.

The primary difference between the two types of law is that common law can be superseded or modified by legislation and can be changed in individual cases by mutual agreement between the parties involved. A violation of common law is not a criminal offense and is handled in a lawsuit as a civil action. Legislated statutes can be changed only by amendment, repeal, or court interpretation.

Employment at will, a common-law principle, has been modified over the years by various statutes. For example, there are laws that prohibit a company from firing or refusing to hire someone for union activity, race, religion, national origin, gender, disability, or age. The right under common law to hire or fire at will is, therefore, restricted in these circumstances.

This principle also means that employment at will can be waived by mutual consent. An employee can sign a contract with the company in which he agrees not to quit and it agrees not to fire him for the duration of the contract. Or a company and a union can agree that no union member will be fired except under the terms of the contract. In both cases, the company has given up its right to employment at will.

Meanings and Gleanings

Employment at will means that the employer has the right, unless restricted by law or contract, to refuse to hire an applicant or to terminate an employee for any reason or for no reason.

Employment Rights

During the past several years, a number of court cases have extended employees' rights that are not covered by specific legislation. Courts in several states have ruled that, although a company's policies-and-procedures manual isn't a formal contract, it can be considered to have the same effect as a contract.

To avoid this type of problem, attorneys advise their clients to specify clearly in their company policy manuals that they are "at-will" employers and to include a statement to that effect on their employment-application forms.

Oral Commitments

Suppose, that during an interview, you told Stella that after a six-month probationary period her job would be permanent. A year later, your company downsizes, and Stella is laid off. She sues. She says, "I left my former job to take this one because the team leader assured me that it was a permanent job." You respond, "I made that comment in good faith. Our company had never had a layoff." Your reply won't be good enough—the court may award Stella a large settlement.

To avoid these types of complications, follow these guidelines:

➤ All managers and team leaders should be trained in procedures concerning termination and adhere to them.

➤ Team leaders or anyone who represents management should never make commitments concerning tenure or other employment conditions orally or in writing.

➤ Make written job offers only after consulting with legal specialists.

➤ Never use the term "permanent employee." *No one* is a permanent employee. If your company must differentiate between temporary and part-time staff members, refer to the full-time people as "regular employees."

➤ On all documents and records relating to employment conditions, state that the company has a policy of employment at will.

Secret Weapon

To avoid legal problems, be sure to have all the facts before you fire someone. Investigate. Get witnesses, and get legal advice.

Nondisciplinary Separation

Every time an employee leaves a company, whether it's voluntary or involuntary, it costs the company a great deal of money. The investment involved in hiring, training, and supervising that person, in addition to the enormous administrative expenses that are incurred, are lost forever. The company loses production output until a replacement is hired and trained, and the interaction among team members is disrupted every time there's a change in the makeup of the group. Team leaders must make every effort to keep turnover down.

Why Good People Quit

Suppose that you've worked hard to build up a team member's skills and that, just when she has become effective, she quits. Or, another employee, who for several years has been one of your steadiest, most reliable workers, comes in one day and gives you his notice. People may leave a job for any number of reasons. Sometimes it's personal: A spouse has to relocate for a job, or someone decides to return to school to pursue a different career. There's not much a team leader can do to reduce turnover based on personal factors.

Often, the reason is job-related. Employees may feel that they aren't making the progress they had hoped for, that their salary is too low, that working conditions are unsatisfactory, or that the job has become boring. In these cases, it's sometimes possible to reduce turnover by identifying recurring problems and correcting them so that other team members don't leave for the same reasons.

Separation Interviews

A *separation interview,* sometimes called an *exit interview,* is designed to help team leaders or supervisors determine the real reasons people leave a job and to obtain information about the company or the job that may have caused discontent. One reason you may be able to get more information during a separation interview is that people often feel freer to open up when they have nothing to lose.

The immediate supervisor should *not* be the one to conduct the exit interview. Usually separation interviews are conducted by the human-resources department. But when teams work in locations that have no human-resource representative, a team leader may be required to interview people who leave another team in that facility. Here are some guidelines for conducting an effective separation interview:

➤ To avoid getting superficial or even misleading reasons from a departing employee, don't ask, "Why are you leaving?" You can develop better information by asking good questions. Ask questions about the job itself:

- What did you like most about the job? Least?
- How do you feel about the progress you've made in this company?
- How do you feel about compensation, benefits, and working conditions?

From the patterns of answers you get from people who are leaving your company, you can gain insight into facets of the job you hadn't realized. If you hear numerous reports of dissatisfaction in specific areas, take action to investigate them; if the reports are valid, correct the problem, or else turnover will continue to climb.

➤ Ask questions about supervision, such as, "How would you describe your team leader's style of leading the team, and how did you react to it?" and "What do you feel were your team leader's strengths and weaknesses?"

It's important to explore the area of employee-supervisor relations because it causes problems in many companies. Feedback from an exit interview makes team leaders aware of factors that may have caused problems so that they can take steps to correct them. They can also learn why they've been commended and be encouraged to reinforce those areas.

➤ Ask questions that might give you insight into other problem areas: "If you could discuss with top management exactly how you feel about this company, what would you tell them?"

This open-ended question often elicits interesting responses. Let employees speak freely. Avoid leading questions, and encourage people to express their true feelings, attitudes, perceptions, fears, and hopes about your organization.

➤ If an employee has accepted a job with another company, ask, "What does your new job offer you that you're not getting here?" The answer may repeat some of the things you've already discussed, but it may also uncover some of the ways your company failed to meet this person's hopes, goals, or expectations.

Secret Weapon

An unbiased, objective separation interview shouldn't be conducted by the supervisor of the employee who is leaving. The interview should be conducted by a member of the human-resources department, another team leader, or another management-level person.

When Employees Quit

Some supervisors and team leaders take an employee's resignation as a personal affront. "How could she do this to me?" Be aware that other team members are carefully monitoring the way you handle this situation. The following suggestions help reduce the confusion that often results when a team member leaves your company:

➤ **Don't blow up.** I once worked for a manager who considered anyone who quit to be disloyal. If someone gave him the courtesy of two weeks' notice, he ordered the person to leave immediately. He then bad-mouthed the employee to everyone in the company. The result was that employees quit without giving notice, which caused serious production problems.

➤ **Agree on a mutually satisfactory departure date.** You may need time to readjust your plans.

➤ **Request a status report on the team member's projects so that you can arrange for others to handle them.** Develop a list of vendors, customers, or other people outside your department that the member interacts with so that you can notify them of the change.

➤ **Contact your human-resources department.** They will arrange for a replacement—either an internal transfer or hiring from outside.

➤ **Let other team members know as soon as you're notified.** Tell them how it will affect their work until someone else is hired.

Short-Term Layoffs

If you work in an industry in which work is done seasonally (construction, certain clothing manufacturing, landscaping, and the automobile industry, for example), you're accustomed to temporary layoffs or furloughs. Workers in these fields expect to be laid off at certain times of the year and plan their lives accordingly. They're usually covered by unemployment insurance or, in some union contracts, additional payments. When the new season begins, most of them are rehired.

Some layoffs are unexpected, however, even though they're temporary. Business may slow down or a company may cut its payroll, for example. Laid-off workers have a reasonable chance of being rehired when business picks up, but they have no guarantee.

Although some people will wait for a recall, many choose to look for other jobs. This situation poses a problem for the company because many experienced workers won't be available when they're needed.

Providing Continuing Benefits

Under the federal law known as COBRA (Consolidated Omnibus Budget Reconciliation Act), employees of companies with 20 or more employees are entitled to maintain their health-insurance coverage for 18 months after they leave a company (disabled people can maintain it for 29 months). The company isn't expected to pay their premiums, however. Former employees who enroll in COBRA must pay the full premium at the same rate the company had been paying (usually considerably less than if they had to purchase individual insurance) plus a small administrative charge. COBRA also provides for continuing health-insurance coverage for survivors of employees who die.

Processing Laid-Off Employees

The administrative details of the separation process in most companies are usually taken care of by the human-resources department. In smaller companies or at branch facilities that have no HR department, a team leader usually handles the process.

Inform the people who are to be laid off at an appropriate time. It's only fair to give adequate notice about when they will be laid off. For temporary layoffs, two weeks is typical; for permanent layoffs, thirty days.

At the time of the separation, follow these guidelines. Using a checklist will ensure that everything is covered.

➤ Discuss the continuation of benefits under COBRA, as discussed earlier in this chapter.

➤ Discuss separation severance pay. No law requires severance pay, but some union contracts do mandate it. Many companies voluntarily give severance pay to laid-off workers. The amount varies from company to company and often within a company by job category. Check your company policy.

➤ If appropriate, discuss the call-back procedure.

➤ If an employee isn't receiving a final paycheck at the same time he or she is leaving the company, specify when it's expected.

➤ If provisions have been made to help laid-off employees seek other jobs, refer the person to whomever is responsible for that function.

➤ Retrieve company property: keys, credit cards, ID cards, tools, and company computers used at home. Change computer log-on IDs and computer passwords.

➤ If an employee has incurred expenses for the company, such as travel and entertainment that have not yet been reimbursed, arrange for prompt attention to this matter.

➤ Answer any questions the employee has.

➤ Arrange for the employee to clean out his or her desk, office, or locker.

➤ Arrange for forwarding of any mail and messages that are received at the company after the employee leaves.

➤ Express your good wishes.

Glossary

affirmative action   A written plan developed by a company to commit to hiring women and minorities in proportion to their representation in the community where the firm at which they work is located. Required of companies that have government contracts in excess of $50,000 and more than 50 employees.

Age Discrimination in Employment Act (ADEA)   As amended, prohibits discrimination against individuals forty years of age or older. Some state laws cover all persons over the age of 18.

Americans with Disabilities Act (ADA)   Prohibits discrimination against people who are physically or mentally challenged.

aptitude test   A test designed to determine the potential of candidates in specific areas, such as mechanical ability, clerical skills, or sales potential. The tests are helpful for screening inexperienced people to determine whether they have an aptitude for the type of work for which a company plans to train them. Most aptitude tests can be administered and scored by following a simple instruction sheet.

arbitration   A process in which two parties present their sides of a problem and an arbitrator decides how the problem should be resolved. See also **mediation.**

behavioral science   The study of how and why people behave the way they do.

benchmarking   A process of seeking organizations that have achieved success in an area and learning about their techniques and methods.

body language   A method people use to communicate—not only by what they say but also by their gestures, facial expressions, and movements.

bona fide occupational qualifications (BFOQ)
Positions for which a company is permitted to specify only a man or only a woman for a job. There must be clear-cut reasons, however, for why only a person of that gender can perform the job.

brainstorming   A technique for generating ideas in which participants are encouraged to voice any idea, no matter how "dumb" or useless it may be. By being allowed to think freely and express ideas without fear of criticism, participants can stretch their minds and make suggestions that may seem worthless but that may trigger in the mind of another participant an idea that has value.

case study   A description of a real or simulated situation presented to trainees for analysis, discussion, and solution; used in graduate schools, seminars, and training programs to enable trainees to work on the types of problems they're most likely to meet on the job. Case studies are often drawn from the experiences of real companies.

channel of communication   The path information takes through the organization. If you want to give information to (or get it from) a person in another department, you first go to your boss, who goes to the supervisor of the other department, who, in turn, goes to the person with the information, who gets it and conveys it back through the same channels. By the time you get the information, it may have been distorted by a variety of interpretations.

Civil Rights Act of 1964   Title VII, as amended, prohibits discrimination in employment on the basis of race, color, sex, religion, and national origin.

COBRA   An acronym for the Consolidated Omnibus Budget Reconciliation Act, in which employees of companies with twenty or more employees are entitled to maintain their health-insurance coverage for 18 months after they leave the company (29 months for people who are disabled at the time they leave). The company isn't expected to pay their premiums. Former employees must pay the full premium at the same rate the company had been paying (usually considerably less than if they had to purchase individual insurance) plus a small administrative charge.

communication   The process by which information, ideas, and concepts are transmitted between persons and groups.

constructive discharge   When an employee quits because of purposeful unfair treatment on the job, it is "constructed" by the courts to be an involuntary termination.

control point   A point in a project at which you stop, examine what has been completed, and correct any errors that have been made (before they blow up into catastrophes).

counseling   A means of helping troubled associates overcome barriers to good performance. With careful listening, open discussion, and sound advice, a counselor helps identify problems, clarify misunderstandings, and plan solutions.

cross training   A method of training team members to perform the jobs of other people on the team so that every member is capable of doing all aspects of the team's work.

decentralization   When the focus of a business is shifted from one central facility where all decisions are made and most of the work is done to localized facilities where, within guidelines, decisions are made and work is performed autonomously.

delegation   A process that enables you to position the right work at the right responsibility level, helping both you and the team members you delegate to expand their skills and contributions, while ensuring that all work gets done in a timely manner by the right person with the right experience or interest in the right area.

documentation   A written description of all disciplinary actions taken by a company to protect it in case of legal actions.

downsize   To lay off employees, primarily when business is slow, so that a company can reduce costs. Downsizing differs from traditional layoffs in that total job categories are eliminated—people who held these jobs have little chance of being rehired. See also **layoff.**

employee assistance program (EAP)   A company-sponsored counseling service. Many companies have instituted these types of programs to help their employees deal with personal problems that interfere with productivity. The counselors aren't company employees; they're outside experts who are retained on an as-needed basis.

employment at will   A legal concept under which an employee is hired and can be fired at the will of the employer. Unless restricted by law or contract, the employer has the right to refuse to hire an applicant or to terminate an employee for any reason or for no reason at all.

Equal Pay Act of 1963   An act which requires that the gender of an employee not be considered in determining salary (equal pay for equal work).

goals/objectives   Interchangeable terms to describe an organization's or individual's desired long-run results.

grievance   A formal complaint, usually based on the violation of a union contract or formal company policy.

gripe An informal complaint about working conditions or other aspects of an employee/company relationship.

halo effect The assumption that, because of one outstanding characteristic, all of an applicant's characteristics are outstanding (that person then "wears a halo").

hot button The one thing in a person's makeup that really gets him or her excited—positively or negatively. (To really reach someone, find that person's hot button.)

intelligence test Like the IQ test administered in schools, this test measures the ability to learn. It varies from brief, simple exercises that can be administered by people with little training to highly sophisticated tests that must be administered by a person with a Ph.D. in psychology.

job analysis The process of determining the duties, functions, and responsibilities of a job (the *job description*) and the requirements for the successful performance of a job (the *job specifications*).

job bank A computerized list of the capabilities of all employees in an organization.

job description A listing of the duties, responsibilities, and results a job requires.

job enrichment Redesigning jobs to provide diversity, challenge, and commitment (and to alleviate boredom).

job instruction training (JIT) A systematic approach to training that has four steps: preparation, presentation, performance, and post-work.

job posting A listing on company bulletin boards of the specifications for an available position. Any employee who is interested can apply. After preliminary screening by the human-resources department, employees who meet the basic requirements are interviewed.

job specifications The requirements an applicant should possess to successfully perform a job.

KITA A kick in the you-know-what.

KRA (key-results area) An aspect of a job in which employees must concentrate time and attention to ensure that they achieve the goals for that job.

lateral thinking Looking at a problem from different angles that may give new insights into its solutions (instead of approaching it by logical thinking).

layoff Termination of employees permanently or for a specific period of time due to lack of work or restructuring of an organization.

leadership The art of guiding people in a manner that commands their respect, confidence, and wholehearted cooperation.

M.O. (method, or mode, of operation) The patterns of behavior a person habitually follows in performing work.

management The process of achieving specific results by effectively using an organization's available resources (money, materials, equipment, information, and employees).

mediation A process in which two parties present their sides and a mediator works with them to reach a mutually satisfactory solution. See also **arbitration**.

mentor A team member assigned to act as counselor, trainer, and "big brother" or "big sister" to a new member.

motivators Factors that stimulate a person to expend more energy, effort, and enthusiasm in a job. See also **satisfiers**.

network To make contacts with managers in other companies to whom you can turn for suggestions and ideas.

objectives See **goals**.

opportunity The combination of being in the right place at the right time and having the ability and desire to take advantage of it.

outsourcing Contracting to outside sources any work that previously had been done in-house. As companies become "leaner and meaner," they outsource activities that can be done more effectively by outside specialists. Some examples are payroll, traffic, training, computer programming, advertising, and certain manufacturing activities.

ownership A feeling that you're a full partner in the development and implementation of a project, committed to its successful achievement.

performance standards The results expected from persons performing a job. For performance standards to be meaningful, every person doing that job should know and accept these standards.

performance test A test that measures how well candidates can do the job for which they apply (for example, operating a lathe, entering data into a computer, writing advertising copy, or proofreading manuscripts). When job performance cannot be tested directly, a company may use written or oral tests about job knowledge.

personality test A test designed to identify personality characteristics that varies from the *Readers Digest*-type quickie questionnaires to highly sophisticated psychological evaluations.

piece work A system of compensation in which earnings are based solely on the number of units produced.

platinum rule "Do unto others as they would have you do unto them."

prioritize To rank tasks, by determining their degree of importance, to accomplish your goals on the job or in your life and in taking action accordingly—putting first things first.

profession   An occupation requiring special training or advanced study in a specialized field. Physicians, lawyers, psychologists, and engineers all have to have advanced education and pass examinations to qualify for certification in their professions.

progressive discipline   A systematic approach to correcting infractions of rules. A typical program has six steps, the first of which is an informal warning. If this step isn't successful, it's followed by (as necessary) a disciplinary interview, a written warning, probation, suspension, and, possibly, termination.

recruit   To seek candidates to be considered for employment, usually done by personnel or human-resources departments.

religious practices   Practices that include, according to the EEOC, not only traditional religious beliefs but also moral and ethical beliefs and any beliefs an individual holds "with the strength of a traditional religious view."

results-oriented evaluation system   A system in which performance expectations are agreed on at the beginning of a period and measured at the end of that period. At that time, new goals are developed, which are to be measured at the end of the next period.

role-playing   A variation of case studies in which participants act out the parts of the characters involved. Used chiefly in studying problems in which interaction between characters is a major aspect.

satisfiers   Also called maintenance factors; the factors—including working conditions, money, and benefits—employees must get from a job in order to expend even minimum effort in performing their work. After employees are satisfied with these factors, however, just giving them more of the same factors doesn't motivate them to work harder. See also **motivators**.

selection   A process of screening applicants to determine their suitability for a position. Preliminary screening is usually done by the human-resources department; subsequent screening is done by supervisors or team leaders.

self-esteem   The way you feel about yourself. If you think of yourself as a success, you will be a success; if you think of yourself as second-rate, you will always be second-rate—unless you change your self-perception. And it *can* be done.

sexual harassment   Any unwelcome sexual advances or requests for sexual favors or any conduct of a sexual nature when an employer makes submission to sexual advances a term or condition of employment, either initially or later on; or when submission or rejection is used as a basis of working conditions, including promotion, salary adjustment, assignment of work, and termination, or has the effect of interfering with an individual's work or creating a hostile or intimidating work environment.

SOPs (standard operating procedures)   A set of standard practices in which company plans and policies are detailed (sometimes called "the company bible").

spontaneous termination   A situation in which an employee is discharged without progressive discipline, usually precipitated by an egregious violation of company rules such as fighting, drunkenness, or gross insubordination. See also **progressive discipline**.

team   A group of people who collaborate and interact synergistically in working toward a common goal.

telecommuting   Technology that enables a person to perform work at home or at a location remote from a central office by receiving assignments and submitting completed work via computer.

training manuals   Handbooks for teaching routine tasks; they make the training process easy for both trainer and trainees and can always be referred to when an employee is in doubt about what to do.

trait system of performance evaluation   A system in which employees are rated on a series of traits, such as quantity and quality of work, attendance, and initiative. Ratings are usually measured on a scale from poor to superior.

Forms

Discipline Worksheet

Part I (Complete before interview begins)

Team member: _____ Date: _____

Offense: _____

_____

_____

Policy and Procedures provision: _____

Date of occurrence: _____

Previous similar offenses: _____

_____

What I want to accomplish: _____

_____

Special considerations: _____

_____

Questions to ask at beginning of interview: _____

_____

_____

PART II (Keep in front of you during interview)

- Keep calm and collected.
- Get the whole story.
- Listen actively.
- Don't interrupt.
- Emphasize the *what,* not the *who.*
- Avoid sarcasm.
- Give *team member* an opportunity to solve the problem.

PART III (Fill out near end of interview)

Suggestions made by team member: _____

_____

_____

Agreed-on solution: _____

_____

_____

PART IV (Action taken: Fill in when interview is finished)

Documentation completed: _____

_____

Termination Checklist

Name of employee: _____ Date: _____

Part I: If discharged for poor performance, steps taken to improve performance:

    Date   Action

_____

_____

Comments: _____

_____

If discharged for poor conduct, list progressive disciplinary steps taken:

    Date   Action

_____ Informal warning

_____ Written warning

_____ Disciplinary interview

_____ Suspension

_____ Other (specify) _____

_____

Comments: _____

_____

Part II

Have you reviewed all pertinent documents? _____

Have you treated this case in the same way as similar cases in the past? _____

Has this action been reviewed by your immediate superior? _____

By human resources department? _____

By legal department? _____

Does employee have any claim pending against company? _____

Any workers' compensation claims? _____

Other (specify): _____

Part III: Termination Interview

Conducted by: _____

Date: _____ Place: _____

Witness: _____

Comments: _____

Final actions: _____

_____

ID and keys returned? _____

Company property returned? _____

Final paycheck issued? _____

Additional comments: _____

_____

Index

A

acceptance, delegated tasks (gaining from team members), 34-35
action plans, writing (performance appraisals), 137
active listening, 104
age discrimination, 90
Age Discrimination in Employment Act of 1967, 78
alcohol and drugs (counseling employees), 142-145
applicants
  finding, 50-51
    application forms, 56
    job fairs, 54
    on-the-job training, 54
    part-time workers, 54
    pushing HR, 51
    routine sources, 52-53
    screening resumes, 55-56
    surfing the Internet, 54
  interview deception, 64-65
  interview dominance, 65-66
  testing, 67-68
  verifying references, 68-69
application forms (finding applicants), 56
appraisal interviews, 133-137
aptitude tests, 67
arbitration, 152
assigning tasks (delegation), 33
at will employment, 174-177
  employee rights, 175-176
  nondisciplinary separation, 177-181
    exit interviews, 178-180
    reacting to employees who quit, 180-181
  oral commitments, 176-177
  short-term layoffs, 181-183
    processing laid-off employees, 182, 183
    providing continuing insurance, 181-182
authority, providing for delegated tasks, 36-37

B

benchmarking, 10
BFOQs (Bona Fide Occupational Qualifications), 82

body language, 105
building self-esteem, 139-142

C

candidate characteristics (hiring), 46-48
Civil Rights Act of 1964, 78
COBRA (Consolidated Omnibus Budget Reconciliation), 181
communication, 97
  assumptions, 106
  body language, 105
  conferences and meetings, 106-110
  knowing your audience, 99
  knowing your subject, 98-99
  listening skills, 101-104
    taking notes, 104
  managing multiple priorities, 40-41
  preconceptions, 106
  speaking skills, 99-101
    listening to your own voice, 100
    visual aids, 100-101
compensation (pay analysis), 48
complaints (counseling employees), 145-150
  checking out complaints, 146-147
  chronic complainers, 146
  correcting problems, 147-148
  formal grievances, 148-149
compromise (job specifications), 47, 48
conducting interviews, 64-66
conferences, 106-110
conflicts, resolving, 150-152
constructive criticism, 135
constructive discharge, 174
continuing insurance, providing, 181-182
control points (delegation), 36
counseling employees, 139
  alcohol and drugs, 142-145
  building self-esteem, 139-142
  complaints, 145-150
  EAPs (Employee Assistance Programs), 154-155
  resolving conflicts, 150-152
  when talking doesn't help, 152-154
counteroffers, 74-75
criteria (performance standards), 124

D

daily activities, planning, 26-28
  prioritization, 26-27
deception (applicant interviews), 64-65
delegating, 37-40
  assigning tasks, 33
  control points, 36
  gaining acceptance, 34-35
  giving instructions, 33-34
  hesitating to do so, 31-37
  multiple priorities, 40-42
    communication, 40-41
    saying no, 42
    work smarter-not harder,
    41
  providing tools and authority,
    36-37
  to teams, 37-38
    multidepartmental teams,
    39-40
diplomacy (facilitation), 2-3
discipline
  disciplinary interviews, 163
  probation, 165-167
  progressive, 158-159
  reprimands, 159-163
    documentation, 163
    excuses, 162
    plan of action, 162
  suspension, 167-168
  termination, 168-172
    employment at will,
    174-177
    human resources
    representatives, 171
    spontaneous, 172-174
  written warnings, 164-165
discrimination
  age, 90
  Americans with Disabilities Act
    (ADA), 90-91
  sexual harrassment, 91-92
documentation
  reprimands, 163
  spontaneous termination,
    173-174
dominance (applicant interviews), 65-66
drugs (counseling employees), 142-145

E

EAPs (Employee Assistance Programs), 154-155
education (job candidates), 46
EEO laws, 77-83
  age discrimination, 90
  Americans with Disabilities Act
    (ADA), 90-91

  BFOQs (Bona Fide Occupational
    Qualifications), 82-90
  lawful and unlawful questions,
    83-89
  sexual harrassment, 91-92
Employee Assistance Programs,
see EAPs
employees
  counseling, 139
    alcohol and drugs, 142-145
    building self-esteem,
    139-142
    complaints, 145-150
    EAPs (Employee Assistance
    Programs), 154-155
    resolving conflicts,
    150-152
  hiring, 43-44
    age discrimination, 90
    Americans with Disabilities
    Act (ADA), 90-91
    candidate characteristics,
    46-48
    interviews, 59-67
    job analyses, 44-46
    making the decision, 69-70
    making the offer, 70-75
    sexual harrassment,
    91-92
    testing applicants,
    67-68
    verifying references,
    68-69
  motivating, 111-114
    getting to know your team,
    113-114
    method of operation
    (M.O.), 112-113
    money as motivation,
    114-118
    plaques and certificates,
    122
    praise, 120-121
    recognition, 118-119
    showing you care,
    119-120
    thank-you cards,
    121-122
  rights, 175-176
employment agencies (finding applicants), 52-53
employment at will, 174-177
  employee rights, 175-176
  nondisciplinary
    separation, 177-181
    exit interviews, 178-180
    reacting to employees who
    quit, 180-181
    short-term layoffs,
    181-183
  oral commitments,
    176-177

equal employment laws, 77-83
  age discrimination, 90
  Americans with Disabilities Act
    (ADA), 90-91
  BFOQs (Bona Fide Occupational
    Qualifications), 82-90
  lawful and unlawful questions,
    83-89
  sexual harrassment, 91-92
Equal Pay Act of 1963, 78
evaluating performance, 123
  appraisal interview,
    133-137
  recording reviews, 137-138
  result-based systems,
    131-133
  standards, setting, 124-127
  trait-based systems, 127-131
exit interviews, 178-180

F

facilitation, 2-3
**final decisions (hiring
  employees), 69-70**
**finding applicants (hiring),
  50-51**
  application forms, 56
  job fairs, 54
  on-the-job training, 54
  part-time workers, 54
  pushing HR, 51
  routine sources, 52-53
  screening resumes, 55-56
  surfing the Internet, 54
**firing someone, *see*
  termination**
flexibility
  goal-setting, 19
  SOPs, 22
formal appraisals
  interviews, 133-137
    constructive
      criticism, 135
    discussing performance,
      133-134
    reviewing goals, 136-137
    soliciting
      comments, 135-136
    writing action
      plans, 137
  performance standards,
    125-127
  recording reviews, 137-138
  result-based systems, 131-133
  trait-based systems, 127-131
formal grievances, 148-149
  preventing, 149

G

goals, 17
  changing, 19-20
  reviewing (performance
    appraisals), 136-137
  setting, 18-19
    attainability, 19
    clarity, 19
    flexibility, 19
    going beyong hopes, 18
    team acceptance, 20-21
Golden Rule, 13-14
grievances, 147
  formal, 148-149
    preventing, 149
**group development
  (teamwork), 4-5**

H

**headhunters (finding appli-
  cants), 52**
**help-wanted ads (finding
  applicants), 52**
hiring employees, 43-44
  age discrimination, 90
  Americans with Disabilities Act
    (ADA), 90-91
  application forms, 56
  candidate characteristics,
    46-48
    compromising job specs,
      47-48
  finding applicants, 50-51
    job fairs, 54
    on-the-job training, 54
    part-time workers, 54
    pushing HR, 51
    routine sources, 52-53
    surfing the Internet, 54
  internal transfers, 49-50
    limitations, 50
  interviews
    conducting, 64-66
    preparing for, 59-60
    questions to ask, 60-63
    taking notes, 66-67
  job analyses, 44-46
    developing job descrip-
      tions, 44-46
  making the decision, 69-70
  making the offer, 70-75
    counteroffers, 74-75
  pay analysis, 48
  recruiting personnel, 48-49
  screening resumes, 55-56
  sexual harrassment, 91-92
  testing applicants, 67-68
  verifying references, 68-69

human resources
finding applicants, 51
recruiting personnel, 48-49
representatives (termination), 171

I

importance vs. urgency, 28
instructions, giving
(delegation), 33-34
insubordination, 173
insurance, providing continuing, 181-182
intelligence tests, 67
internal transfers (hiring), 49-50
limitations, 50
Internet (finding applicants), 54
interviews
conducting, 64-66
applicant deception, 64-65
applicant dominance,
65-66
taking notes, 66-67
disciplinary, 163
exit, 178-180
performance appraisals,
133-137
constructive
criticism, 135
discussing performance,
133-134
reviewing goals, 136-137
soliciting comments,
135-136
writing action plans, 137
preparing for, 59-60
questions to ask, 60-63

J-K

job descriptions (hiring), 44-46
job fairs (finding applicants), 54
job offers, making, 70-75
counteroffers, 74-75

KRAs (key results areas), 132

L

laws (equal employment), 77-83
age discrimination, 90
Americans with Disabilities Act
(ADA), 90-91
BFOQs (Bona Fide Occupational
Qualifications), 82-90
lawful and unlawful questions,
83-89
sexual harrassment, 91-92

layoffs, short-term, 181-183
listening, 101-104
taking notes, 104

M

meditation, 150-152
meetings, 106-110
micromanagement, 37
money as motivation, 114
motivators vs. satisfiers,
114-118
motivation, 111-114
method of operation (M.O.),
112-113
getting to know your team,
113-114
money as, 114
motivators vs. satisfiers,
114-118
plaques and
certificates, 122
praise, 120-121
recognition, 118-119
sample interview
questions, 62
showing you care, 119-120
thank-you cards, 121-122
multidepartmental teams,
delegating tasks to, 39-40

N-P

nondisciplinary separation,
177-181
note-taking
conducting interviews, 66-67
listening skills, 104

offers, making (hiring
employees), 70-75
counteroffers, 74-75
on-the-job training (finding
applicants), 54
oral commitments, 176-177
organization (teamwork), 3-5

part-time workers (finding
applicants), 54
pay analysis, hiring, 48
performance, 14
evaluating, 123
appraisal interview,
133-137
recording reviews, 137-138
result-based systems,
131-133
standards, setting, 124-127
trait-based systems, 127-131
tests, 67